WERE
YOU
THERE?

STATIONS OF THE CROSS

FR. FRANCIS MAPLE O.F.M CAP

McCRIMMONS
Great Wakering, Essex

First Published for Francis Maple in Great Britain in 1999 by
McCRIMMON PUBLISHING COMPANY LIMITED.
10–12 High Street, Great Wakering, Essex SS3 0EQ, England.
Telephone (01702) 218956 Fax (01702) 216082
Email: mccrimmons@dial.pipex.com

© 1999 Francis Maple

ISBN 0 85597 607 1

All Scripture quotations are taken from the Jerusalem Bible
published and copyright 1966, 1967 and 1968 by Darton, Longman & Todd Ltd
and Doubleday & Co. Inc. and used by permission of the publishers.

Typeset by McCrimmons in Palatino and Garamond ITC
Cover design: Brendan Waller
Colour reprographics: Anagram Litho Ltd, Southend-on-Sea, Essex
Printed by Antony Rowe Limited.

Contents

Introduction

If you had been in Jerusalem on the day of Christ's crucifixion, how would you have acted? Would you have followed Him closely, like John and Mary, or would you have kept your distance, like Peter? With this book, you have the opportunity to walk, in your imagination, with a variety of characters from the Gospel story, considering the events from their points of view.

When I was a Parish Priest at Penmaenmawr in North Wales we made the Stations of the Cross three times a week during Lent. I was looking for a way to make this much-loved Franciscan devotion a little more varied, and so I wrote the versions collected together in this book. They have all been tried and tested on parishioners and well-received.

Each version of the Stations is suitable for public use in Church. They are also a helpful aid to private meditation.

F. Francis Maple O.F.M.Cap.

Fr. Francis Maple O.F.M. Cap.

Walking with Jesus on the Way of the Cross

INTRODUCTION

In the beginning of the book it is written, "Behold I come to do your will, O God." It is the will of my Father that I should suffer, die and rise again to open the gates of heaven for my sinful sisters and brothers. Those gates were closed to them because of the disobedience of their first parents, Adam and Eve, who were tempted and lured away from God by Satan, the archdeceiver. I, Jesus, your elder brother, now invite you to accompany me on this painful journey I endured for love of you. Let me assure you that if I had to face the same trials again just to save one of you, I would do it willingly with all the love in my heart.

1. JESUS IS CONDEMNED TO DEATH

"Behold the man!" With these words Pilate leads me out to face the crowd. Isaiah wrote of me that in my sufferings I would be no man but a worm. Truly I am a physical wreck. Oh, Jerusalem, the city that murders the prophets and stones the messengers sent to her! These are my own people who are clamouring for my death, but I feel such compassion for them. They are like sheep without a shepherd. Those who should have guided them failed them. Caiaphas, their High Priest, was stubborn and unteachable; he could not accept that I am God's Son, the Messiah. He denounced me as a blasphemer. That fox, Herod, had hardened his conscience and as a king was not a good example to his people. Pontius Pilate was cowardly; he knows I am innocent of any crime, but he is afraid for his own safety, so now he hands me over to be crucified and allows Barabbas, thief and murderer, to go free. How well I understand their motives and their weaknesses! But they are all children of my Father. They have no power over me. No-one takes my life from me, I lay it down myself by my own will and the will of my Father. This is the cup my Father has given me, and I shall drink it.

2. JESUS RECEIVES HIS CROSS

When I prayed last night in the Garden of Gethsemane I foresaw the suffering and death I would have to face, but it is still a shock when the soldiers place the cross on my shoulder. It is heavy, and I stagger for a moment as I take hold of the rough wood with both hands. I know that I shall need all my physical strength to carry this cross to Calvary; but I take it up willingly and gladly, because I know that it will be the means of winning salvation for all my sisters and brothers. I take the place of Barabbas and of all sinners. Two thieves are sharing this journey with me. I shall pray for them and try to support them.

3. JESUS FALLS THE FIRST TIME

Already I feel weak and sick. The scourging I received from the Roman soldiers took its toll on my body and I lost a lot of blood. I fall to my knees, jolting the cross against my shoulder. The weight of the cross presses me down, and I can feel the sins of all my brothers and sisters, past, present and future. I think especially of those who fall into sin in their early lives. The temptations of the world and of Satan are so strong, and young people are so vulnerable. Their hearts are good, but they can so easily be corrupted by bad example, or bad company, or the ridicule of their peers, so that they are led away from their heavenly Father. I love them all, and I pray that they will receive the strength to remain faithful. For their sake, I struggle to my feet.

4. JESUS MEETS HIS SORROWFUL MOTHER

Now my beloved mother is here, making her way through the crowd to meet me. I've being wanting to get close to her on this journey. There's no need for me to tell her that I love her. She knows that, but I just want to touch her to give her strength and to be strengthened by her presence. How sad she looks, and how brave she is. She places her hand on my arm. She is full of love and sympathy for me. As I look into her eyes I remember all that we've shared together during our lives. She looked after me so tenderly when I was a child. She was there, encouraging me, when I performed my first miracle. She was often puzzled by the things I said and did, but she never stopped loving me and trusting in God. It was through her faith that I was able to come into the world to save my poor sinful people, and I know she will stay close to me until the end. I think of all the people in generations to come who will love me and love my mother. Now, our brief moment together is over, and the soldiers are hurrying me away, but I know my mother is still following me.

5.   THE CROSS IS LAID UPON SIMON OF CYRENE

The soldiers are anxious, because I am making slow progress. They are afraid that I will not be able to complete this journey alone, so they have picked out a man in the crowd to help me carry my cross. His name is Simon, a Cyrenian. Poor Simon! He doesn't want to get involved, and I understand, but the soldiers leave him no option. He approaches me resentfully at first. I have to help him to appreciate how important this task is, and how greatly I value his assistance. I touch him gently and immediately a change comes over him. Now he realises that if I am with him the yoke is easy and the burden is light. He takes up his cross willingly. I pray that all my sisters and brothers will have the courage to take up their own crosses and follow me. I can give them the strength they need.

6.   VERONICA WIPES THE FACE OF JESUS

The heat of the day is exhausting and I can feel sweat and blood trickling down my face and into my eyes. I glance at my two companions and I can see that they are suffering, too. Their faces are smeared with sweat and dirt. Now a woman comes towards me out of the crowd. I can feel the goodness and generosity in my heart. She brings a clean towel which she has dipped in cool water and she begins to wipe my face. It refreshes and revives me. As she removes the towel from my face I smile at her and give her such a loving look of thanks, one she will never forget. Whenever she will pray she need only close her eyes and she will recall that loving glance. A soldier pulls her away and I see her looking at the towel. She's surprised to see the image of my face imprinted on it. She looks towards me questioningly and once again I give her a smile.

7. JESUS FALLS THE SECOND TIME

I'm getting weaker. My head is throbbing with this migraine headache I have. I can scarcely see where I am going. It's such an effort to keep my eyes open. The waves of nausea make me dizzy and I fall again. I'm half way through this journey and I think of all those in middle age who fall and stumble on their way through life. Those like me who grow tired and weary of the monotony of living. Those who are overwhelmed with depression or despair, those who despair, those who fear they are lost and feel they have achieved nothing in life. I think and pray for all of them at this fall, and I want them to witness that through my rising they too can overcome, with my help, all these trials and setbacks.

8. JESUS MEETS THE DAUGHTERS OF JERUSALEM

There have been many people who have met me. They've listened to my words and even followed me for a while. Many have been attracted to me for what they can get from me. How many have really loved me for myself? I can see these women of Jerusalem openly wailing at seeing me. I've met them before. I know they genuinely love me for myself. They have come to show their sorrow. I'm grateful to them. Their love eases my suffering. I can see in the future what suffering they will have to face. Not many years from now in the year 70, the Romans will come and butcher their children, destroy their homes and pull down their beloved temple. I feel for them at this moment. I want to warn them of their plight and tell them to weep not for me but for themselves and their children. They don't understand but they know that I love them. Now I feel the point of a soldier's lance moving me on.

9. JESUS FALLS THE THIRD TIME

How many journeys I've made on foot. Sometimes I've been tired and exhausted, but I've always reached my destination. This journey is by far the hardest, longest and most painful of my life and it is one destination, with my Father's help, I'm most definitely going to reach. Like a marathon runner who has hit that brick wall, I keep telling myself, just one more step, just one more step. Each step gets me nearer the winning post. It is the thought of what I shall achieve on the hill of Calvary, the obedience to my Father's will and the salvation of my sisters and brothers that makes me take each step. I now can see the hill and my foot stumbles and I fall again. I lie on the ground exhausted. I could die at this moment and I think of all those nearing the end of their lives who will be tempted to give up the struggle of living. Those who are weary of life, and cannot see the light at the end of the tunnel. Those who are weighted down in old age with physical disabilities and mental infirmities. Those who see life pointless and feel themselves no longer useful. I pray that, like me, they will persevere to the bitter end. Like my brother Paul I hope they will all be able to say, "I have fought the good fight. I have won the race. I now await the crown that awaits me." I appeal to my Father to help me and He give me that strength I need to get to my feet and finish this journey.

10. JESUS IS STRIPPED OF HIS GARMENTS

What a relief it is to have the cross taken from my shoulder. The greatest physical pain I've had to bear is this wound to my shoulder. The friction of the rough wood has torn my flesh down to the bone. The burning pain plays on my mind. Now two soldiers roughly pull the clothes from my back. The pain is excruciating. Some of my wounds have stuck to my clothing and the removal of them has caused my wounds to reopen. Here I stand naked to the gaze of all present. I cast a glance at my mother and friends and I can see how shocked and embarrassed they are. All I can do is pray for them.

11. JESUS IS NAILED TO THE CROSS

Very quickly two soldiers drag me down and lay me on my cross. I stretch out my arms. I know what is to follow. At the Garden of Gethsemane I dreaded this moment and it caused me to sweat drops of blood. As they drive the nails through my wrists and feet I hold my breath and try not to scream in agony. Each blow of the hammer causes me to flinch and I know I can only endure this pain because I am conscious of my Father's help and this burning love I have to save everyone. I hope that whenever people think of this moment they will realise the evil and horror of sin, and what sin achieved and made me suffer. I've been fastened to the cross and now it s the turn of my fellow prisoners. I can hear them wailing and I know exactly what they are going through. I'm sharing their fear and their pain and I pray for them to be given the same strength that was given to me. My cross is now raised and with a jolt is secured in the ground. And now my body hangs painfully from my pierced wrists. Those passing by mock me and say, "If you are Christ come down from the cross and we'll believe you." I whisper, "Father, forgive them for they know not what they do."

12. Jesus dies on the cross

Hanging in this position I can't breath. I feel suffocated. I can hear the thief on my left cursing me and demanding that I save myself and Him. The thief on my right reproaches him and tells him I'm innocent and to stop tormenting me. I have been praying to win these criminals over to me and one of them now responds to my grace. He says, "Jesus, remember me when you come into your kingdom." Slowly and painfully I turn my head in his direction and with joy I can say to Him, "Friend, I promise you this very day you will be with me in paradise."

Time is passing and I can see the sky darkening. Some of the onlookers realising that a storm is about to break scurry away. But my mother and faithful friends remain. I still have one last treasure that I have not given away. That's my mother. I shall now make her the mother of all God's children. With great difficulty I whisper, "Woman, behold thy son." Then I look at John and say, "Behold your mother." Some will think that I should have made provision for my mother before this, but I deliberately chose this moment of my sacrifice precisely because of the important part she has played in the salvation of the world.

My mouth is parched and my throat is sore. My tongue is swollen and feels like dry leather. I can feel myself losing consciousness, and I quietly murmur, "I thirst." A kind man quickly brings a sponge soaked in vinegar and presses it to my lips, and the bitter taste revives me a little. What I really thirst for is love.

A great darkness has now descended. But it's nothing compared with the darkness and desolation in my soul. My Father wants me to share all that His sinful children have to endure. Whenever they sin, they feel the pain of separation from God and imagine that He has abandoned them. I'm now feeling what they must feel. I've hit rock bottom. I can't fall any lower. This has to be the lowest ebb of my life. I can't bear to think that even for a split second I should feel abandoned and apart from my Father, and I cry out, "My God, my God, why have you deserted me?"

I now feel that the end is near. I look back on my life and I know I could not have loved my Father more and all those He has given to me. With utmost satisfaction I can say, "It is finished."

Every Jewish mother taught her child the night prayer, 'Into your hands I commend my spirit.' I now offer my spirit to my Father and I know with what love He will receive me. "Father, into your hands I commend my spirit." With those words I bow my head and die. [Pause.]

Not long after this the centurion was ordered to break the legs of the prisoners and have their bodies taken down from the cross. This was done to the two thieves. But finding me already dead one soldier pierced my side with a lance and immediately water and blood flowed out. In fulfilment of Scripture, not one bone of my body was broken and they looked upon the one they pierced.

13. JESUS IS TAKEN DOWN FROM THE CROSS

As soon as my soul leaves my body I descend to that place where all the just souls who have died await my presence to take them to heaven. Adam and Eve eagerly receive the good news I give them that I have won salvation for them and all their children. I am so happy to be reunited with my foster father Joseph. I wish you could experience the joy of that moment.

My two secret friends Joseph of Arimathea and Nicodemus, and John, my beloved disciple, take my body down from the cross. They place it in the lap of my mother. How tenderly she treats it. Carefully she removes the crown of thorns from my head and with the women helping her she anoints my body for burial. They have to hurry because the Sabbath is due to begin.

14. JESUS IS LAID IN THE SEPULCHRE

Having completed the anointing my friends carry my body to be buried to rest in peace. Joseph has very kindly given to Mary his own tomb in which to bury my body. Mary, my mother, and the women linger awhile not wanting to leave. Very reluctantly they draw away and it takes the three men to roll the stone across the entrance of the tomb. As they leave guards take up their position because the priests remember me saying that I shall rise on the third day. They fear that there may be a possibility that my disciples will come and steal my body away.

15. Jesus rises from the dead

Not one of my disciples believed what I had told them, about my rising on the third day. They had heard me tell them several times that I would suffer and die. On hearing this they would block their ears, and in doing so they never heard what was to follow, that I would rise on the third day. Only my mother accepted this truth and awaited my resurrection. In the early hours of the third day I rose from the dead and together with all the just, who had died before me, went to heaven to meet my Father and the Holy Spirit. The welcome given us by the angelic host was triumphant. I now eagerly await you, my friends, to join me.

The Way of the Cross with Mary

INTRODUCTION

Jesus, my Son, when you were forty days old your foster father Joseph and I presented you in the temple to your heavenly Father. There the holy man Simeon took you in his arms and said, "This child is destined for the fall and for the rising of many in Israel, destined to be a sign that is rejected – and a sword will pierce your own soul too." On this journey that we are going to make, yes, a sword pierced my heart, but it was nothing to what you, God's Son and my Son, endured for your brothers and sisters.

1. JESUS IS CONDEMNED TO DEATH

I am Mary, the mother of the condemned man, Jesus. My son is on trial although He has never done any harm to anyone. He is kindness and goodness itself. Even Pontius Pilate, the Roman governor, could find no fault in Him, yet here He is being led out to execution. Listen to the crowd cheering. These people He loved so much, the same people who, only last week, were shouting 'Hosanna' and spreading palms in front of Him, now they are clamouring for his death. How fickle people can be! Pilate gave them a chance to save Him, but they chose instead Barabbas, a notorious criminal. How could anyone be preferred to my Son?

Prayer: Jesus, my Son, you never defended yourself when Pilate was so weak and cowardly, thinking only of himself. I pray for all those like him today who act in cowardice and fear.

2. JESUS RECEIVES HIS CROSS

My heart goes out to my Son. He is already weak and ill, having been scourged, crowned with thorns and deprived of food and sleep. He staggers under the weight of the cross and I long to run to Him, but the crowd prevents me. I wish I could help Him, but I know it is the will of the Father that He should carry this cross. My cross is to have to stand by and witness His suffering. See how calmly He accepts the cross, because this is the way He will bring salvation to all these people.

Prayer: Jesus, my Son, I am grateful to know that there are people in this world who willingly carry the cross, who beg you to be allowed to help you carry your cross. They know the value of the cross, that God's will is for their best. I pray that more of my children would understand this.

3. JESUS FALLS THE FIRST TIME

Jesus falls to His knees, unable to support the weight of the cross on His shoulder. I think of the times during His childhood when He would fall and hurt Himself. He always ran to me to make it better, and I was always there to comfort Him. Now, He is in real pain and I, His mother, can do so little for Him.

Prayer; Jesus, my Son, I now have your brothers and sisters to look after, and they fall and stumble through sin many times. I pray for you to give them the grace to realise what a loving mother I am and how I long for them to come to me for solace, comfort and strength. I am always here in their time of need.

4. JESUS MEETS HIS MOTHER

At last I manage to get through the crowd for a moment and reach my Son. I know this may be the last time I can touch him. He turns and looks at me, and His eyes are full of pain, but also of love. I am so glad He prepared me for this moment. How I would love to be able to hold Him to my heart for one more time, but it's impossible. Now I can really appreciate those words of the old man Simeon, "And a sword will pierce your own soul." Jesus doesn't say a word, but I know my presence strengthens Him, as He strengthens me. My brief moment with my Son is over and a soldier brushes me aside.

Prayer: Jesus, my Son, my heart goes out at this moment to all mothers whose sons have not lived up to their standards, who turn their backs on their mothers. They are not like you. I feel for those mothers. Let them know they will always find strength and understanding from me.

5. THE CROSS IS LAID UPON SIMON OF CYRENE

It was obvious even to those Roman soldiers that Jesus could not continue alone. Suddenly, they drag a man out of the crowd and they are making him take one end of the huge wooden cross. Who is this stranger? Someone says his name is Simon. Whoever he is, I bless him for helping my Son.

Prayer: Jesus, my Son, help your brothers and sisters to realise that when they help anyone in need they are helping you to carry your cross, because you have said, "In so far as you did this to one of the least of these brothers of mine, you did to me."

6. VERONICA WIPES THE FACE OF JESUS

The day is so hot and the road is steep and dusty. I can see blood and sweat running down Jesus' face and into His eyes so that He can hardly see His way. But now another stranger appears. A woman called Veronica has taken pity on Him, and she bravely comes forward with a cool damp towel with which she carefully wipes His face. As always, my dear Son rewards even the smallest acts of kindness. He gives her a look of love and gratitude she will never forget. And when she takes her towel away she finds the image of His face imprinted on it.

Prayer: Jesus, my Son, I am grateful for all those people, like Veronica, who never think of themselves and only think of others: missionaries, nurses, doctors, those who care for the homeless and handicapped and many others like them. Bless them and reward them, and increase their number.

7. JESUS FALLS THE SECOND TIME

Jesus is forcing Himself to go on, one painful step at a time. The hot sun makes Him dizzy, His head must be aching, His wounds must be on fire. He loses his footing for a moment and He falls a second time. He is half way through His journey. I wonder how much more He can bear, but I never doubt that He will see it through.

Prayer: Jesus, my Son, I pray for all those people who reach middle age crisis and do not know where to find strength to cope with life and continue the journey. As a mother, I feel for them and I pray for them. Inspire them to overcome this crisis.

8. JESUS MEETS THE WOMEN OF JERUSALEM

A group of women push to the front of the crowd to get closer to my Son. Unlike most of the onlookers, they really feel sorry for Him, and they are weeping openly. I recognise some of these women. They once brought their children to Him to be blessed. He pauses for a while, touched by their sympathy for Him, but His concern is not for Himself, it is for them. "Do not weep for me; weep rather for yourselves and for your children," He tells them. He knows what is to become of them, and of Jerusalem. That is just like my Son. He doesn't think of Himself, only of others.

Prayer: Jesus, my Son, there is nothing so unique and special as a mother's love. Bless all mothers throughout the world. I thank our Heavenly Father for those mothers who are doing an excellent job, and I pray for those who are having difficulties, who find the burden of motherhood weighing heavily upon them. Help them to realise there is someone who understands their difficulties, and that is me. Let them turn to me for love and strength and inspiration.

9. JESUS FALLS THE THIRD TIME

My poor Son is completely exhausted and aching in every limb. I can feel all His pain. He is almost at the top of the hill now, and the sight of that dreadful place makes Him stumble for a moment and He falls again. Still He doesn't give up. I know it is love for His Father and for His sinful brothers and sisters that makes Him pick Himself up and make one last effort.

Prayer: Jesus, my Son, I pray for all my children that they will persevere to the very end. I know life can be so hard for them, but if, like you, they could see what our Heavenly Father has to offer them they would pick themselves up and through thick and thin reach their goal.

10. Jesus is stripped of His garments

At last my Son has reached the hill of Calvary, now He is going to need all the strength He can muster to face this most cruel death. First, He is to be humiliated. The soldiers pull off His robe, that fine robe I made for Him myself, and He is exposed to the jeering crowd and the embarrassment of the women. The wounds on His back are re-opened, and the cross has rubbed His shoulder down to the bone. How I want to hold Him in my arms and comfort Him!

Prayer: Jesus, my Son, your garments were roughly torn from your body, but sadly there are so many in this world who have no respect for their bodies, no modesty, and for whim or money are so quick to discard their clothing and lead others into sin. I pray for them.

11. Jesus is nailed to the cross

My innocent Son is pulled to the ground and laid on the cross. One soldier puts his foot on Jesus' hand while another soldier hammers a nail into His wrist. I cannot bear to watch any more and I turn away. Now I feel an arm round my shoulders. It is John, Jesus' friend, the beloved disciple. The dreadful hammer blows continue until Jesus is fastened to the cross. Then, as we turn to look, the cross is hoisted up and with a great jolt is secured in the hole in the ground prepared for it. This tears even further the wounds already made by the nails. The pain my Son is enduring must be excruciating. What has He done to deserve this agony?

Prayer: Jesus, my Son, if all those who think lightly of sin could witness what you went through at that moment they would think twice about sinning. May the image of you being nailed to the cross make an impact on their lives, and so make them sin no more.

12. Jesus dies on the cross

Three hours have gone by. People are losing interest now and starting to drift away, back to their work or their homes. A handful of faithful friends remain, and four Roman soldiers waiting for the end. My Son has suffered terribly during these three hours. The pain in His chest makes breathing difficult and speaking almost impossible, yet with His last breath He wants to show His love for us all. Some passers by taunt Him, saying, "So you would destroy the temple and rebuild it in three days? Come down off the cross and then we'll believe you." Jesus simply prays for them: "Father, forgive them; they do not know what they are doing."

Right up to the last moment Jesus thinks of me, His mother. He looks down with such love as He asks me to be a mother to John, and asks John to take care of me and treat me as his mother. I understand what Jesus wants me to do: He wants me to be a mother to all those He loves.

How fitting that his very last words should be the night prayer I taught him, the prayer all Jewish mothers teach their children: "Father, into your hands I commit my spirit." With those words He bowed His head and died. Jesus, I am so pleased that now all your suffering is over. I know you will rise on the third day. This is what you told me and I can't wait to see you again.

Prayer: Jesus, my Son, as you bow your head and die, I pray for all my children in their last agony, that through a good life they need not fear death. Just as I am present at your death may I be present at theirs and commend their lives into their Father's hands.

13. JESUS IS TAKEN DOWN FROM THE CROSS

And so my beloved Son is dead. He is taken down from the cross and laid in my lap. I hold Him tenderly, as I used to do when He was a child. I pull the thorns gently from His head. Touch His matted hair. How many times I have washed and brushed His hair! I caress His face and His wounds. I remember the many times I used to bath him and dress Him in clean clothes. It breaks my heart to see His body now, bearing the marks of so much suffering.

Prayer: Jesus, my Son, I can appreciate how those mothers feel who see their children tragically die. My heart bleeds for them. Inspire them to think of me at this moment, for I can understand and comfort them.

14. JESUS IS LAID IN THE TOMB

Joseph of Arimathea, a secret disciple and a wealthy man, has had permission from Pilate to take my Son's body for burial. Nicodemus has brought a mixture of spices to anoint my Son's body. His body has to be anointed hurriedly because it is almost the Sabbath.

Joseph has wrapped Him in a clean cloth and placed Him in a fresh tomb cut out of the rock, in a garden not far from here. John came with me, and the two Mary's, and we have seen where He is buried. The tomb is now sealed with a huge stone.

Prayer: Jesus, my Son, I eagerly await the resurrection. All that you have done has been so worthwhile. The cost was great but the crown is rewarding. I pray for all my children. My heart aches to think that I should lose one of them. There are others who are not lost but who are suffering the torments of purgatory longing to be united to you and me. I beg you to show them mercy and bring them speedily to their home in heaven. Through the merits of your passion may they, too, be crowned in glory.

CONCLUSION

In response to Mary's prayer for her children in purgatory, let us say the powerful prayer that Jesus Himself gave to St. Gertrude. He promised that whenever this prayer is recited He would release many souls from purgatory. The prayer is, "Eternal Father, I offer you the most precious blood of your divine Son Jesus, in union with all the holy Masses being offered today throughout the world for the Holy Souls in purgatory."

The Way of the Cross with Peter

Lord Jesus, in following your journey to Calvary, may we come to appreciate the depth of your love in suffering the cruellest of all deaths for us. Today, we make this journey in the company of Peter, your chief apostle.

1.   JESUS IS CONDEMNED TO DEATH

I am Peter, a follower of Jesus, and I am heartily ashamed of myself. I was the one who said to Jesus, "I am ready to go with you to prison and death," yet, after He was arrested I was so frightened that I denied even knowing Him. How well Jesus knew me! There, in the High Priest's house, I disowned Him.

The chief priests have brought Jesus to Pilate to see if he will convict Him. Here am I, creeping back secretly to see what is happening. I keep myself hidden, though I'm sure Jesus knows where I am. He has the power to save Himself, if He wants to. I know the power He possesses. I was there when He calmed the storm on the Sea of Galilee. We all thought we would drown, but Jesus told the wind to be still, and the storm ceased immediately. He isn't using that power now. He just gives Himself into the hands of those who want to kill Him. There is a threatening crowd outside, yelling, "Crucify Him!" So Pilate gives in to them, and releases that criminal Barabbas instead. What a coward Pilate is! But am I any different from him?

2.   JESUS RECEIVES HIS CROSS

The cross is laid on Jesus' shoulders and He does nothing to resist. He will not defend Himself, just as He would not allow us to defend Him when the officers of the temple came to arrest Him. Just a few hours ago, I was the brave one, drawing my sword to cut off the ear of the High Priest's servant. But once I was alone with time to think, my courage left me. Now Jesus is being brave. He accepts this punishment willingly, but there is a sad expression on His face as He scans the crowd, looking for His friends. I once told Jesus I would never leave Him. Where else would I go? Now He is alone, apart from two thieves who are to be crucified alongside Him. Perhaps the rest of His friends are somewhere in the midst of this crowd but, like me, they are keeping out of sight. Only John, His beloved disciple, stays close to Him, along with His mother, Mary.

3. JESUS FALLS THE FIRST TIME

It tortures me to see Jesus fall under that heavy cross. I remember the first time I showed weakness. It was in the house of Caiaphas, the High Priest, where Jesus was being interrogated. I was sitting warming myself by the fire, when one of the serving maids said to me, "You were with the man from Nazareth." I immediately replied, "Woman, I do not know the man." How Jesus must have suffered then, knowing that I had turned my back on Him. But now He is on His feet again; He knows what He must do, and He is determined to carry it through.

4. JESUS MEETS HIS MOTHER

A huge crowd has turned out to see this crucifixion. They've all heard about Jesus the Messiah, and they want to see what will happen to Him. As I follow the procession at a distance, I can see Mary again in front of me, making her way through the mob to put her arms around her Son just for a moment. I'm keeping out of sight, knowing that I deserve nothing but reproach from this gentle mother. I visited Mary's home many times. I shared meals there, and she always welcomed me with kindness and generosity, accepting me as one of Jesus' friends. How must she feel, seeing her Son alone, tortured and bleeding? I know how much she loves Him, and I can see that even in this brief meeting Jesus takes comfort from her love and faith in Him. He needs my comfort, too, and I lack the courage to give it to Him.

5. THE CROSS IS LAID UPON SIMON OF CYRENE

Jesus is becoming weaker, and he cannot support the cross on His own. Suddenly, the procession comes to a halt and a couple of Roman soldiers pull a man out of the crowd. He struggles at first, but now they are making him help Jesus carry His cross. It should have been me. Jesus has been such a good friend to me, and now I ought to be helping Him. I'm strong enough to do it, but I lack the courage to come forward, and this stranger has taken what should really be my place. Jesus looks at the man gratefully, as if He knows He can depend on him. I know that look so well. Jesus can put confidence into anyone, and now this stranger, who has become His friend, shoulders the cross cheerfully. Someone in the crowd calls out the man's name: Simon. The name I had before Jesus called me Peter. Well, Simon, at this moment you are a true friend to Jesus.

6. VERONICA WIPES THE FACE OF JESUS

Even in this pitiful condition, Jesus still draws people to Him. As He makes His way slowly and painfully up the hill, a woman watching the procession runs to fetch a cloth with which to wipe His face. She pays no attention to the soldiers who are guarding the prisoners, but goes straight to Jesus, gently placing the cloth to His face and wiping away the sweat and the blood. This is the same Jesus who, just a few days ago, took a towel and knelt down to wash my feet. This woman may never have seen Him before. She may not know who He is. But something inspired her to make this kind gesture, and, of course, Jesus repays all kindness many times over. She unfolds her cloth, and there is Jesus' face imprinted on it. As the soldiers hurry the prisoners away, I can see the woman looking in amazement at the towel and gazing up to take another look at Jesus, trying to understand what is happening.

7. JESUS FALLS THE SECOND TIME

Even with Simon's help, Jesus has to try desperately hard to put one foot in front of the other. He stumbles and falls again. I can see the pain He is suffering, and the sadness, too. I remember that servant in the High Priest's house who challenged me, saying, "You are also one of them, the followers of Jesus." Thinking only of my own safety, I replied indignantly, "No, I am not." I can see now that it was my denial that pushed Jesus to the ground. I have helped to place this burden on His shoulders. I have added to His suffering. But He still won't give up, and now once more He is on His feet and continuing His painful journey.

8.   JESUS MEETS THE WOMEN OF JERUSALEM

Jesus slowly makes His way forward, but now the procession is halted again by a crowd of women showing their sympathy for Him. His concern is all for them, as He tells them to weep for themselves and to be prepared for frightening events to come. I wonder what He means? There were so many times when Jesus tried to prepare us for the future, but we didn't always listen carefully, nor understand what He was saying. It's the same for these women. Jesus longed to gather Jerusalem's children to Him, like a hen gathering her brood under her wings, but they would not let Him. Now it's too late.

9.   JESUS FALLS THE THIRD TIME

Jesus is almost at the end of the journey. His strength fails Him and He falls again. He is physically exhausted, but I know His determination so well. When we all walked with Him on His preaching mission, He used to urge us to keep going from town to town, no matter how tired or discouraged we were. Now, as He gets to His feet again, I remember the third time I let Him down. Another servant in the High Priest's house noticed me and said, "Of course, this man was with Jesus. By his accent he is a Galilean." I turned on him impatiently, saying, "I don't know what you are talking about!" That was the third time I denied Jesus. I had been angry when Jesus said that I would deny Him three times before cockcrow. How right He was for after that denial the cock crew, and at that moment Jesus was led out of the hall. As He passed me He gave me such a look of sadness and love that I could only run outside, weeping bitterly. I know now what pain I have caused my Master.

10. Jesus is stripped of His garments

The soldiers heartlessly drag the clothes from the prisoners' backs. I feel such rage when I see Jesus treated in this way. He is not a criminal like the other two and He doesn't deserve all this. His hands and His shoulders are bleeding, and His feet are sore and dirty from the dusty road. I want to go to Him and shield Him from this mockery, but still something holds me back, I can't trust myself any more. I always thought I was so strong and brave, but now I've been shown just how weak I really am. Will I ever learn that I cannot rely on myself? I need the support and strength of Jesus.

11. Jesus is nailed to the cross

I once saw Jesus at work in the carpenter's shop in Nazareth when He mended some furniture for His mother. He's a skilled craftsman, and He enjoyed making useful and beautiful things with His carpentry tools. What a contrast with the work of these Roman soldiers who are coming now with their hammers and nails to inflict on Jesus the most terrible torture. As they drive the nails through His wrists and His feet, splintering the bone, they seem scarcely to notice the pain they are causing. To them, it is just another day's work. At last, the three crosses are erected and secured, so that the weight of the men's bodies hangs from their arms. Jesus doesn't cry out, but bears even this agony in silence.

12. Jesus dies on the cross

For three hours, Jesus has been dying slowly and painfully. The air is still and heavy, as if a storm is coming. It makes the onlookers uneasy, and they start to drift away. The two Mary's remain, with John, who is trying to comfort Jesus' mother. As people pass Jesus they jeer at Him, saying, "If you are really the Messiah, save yourself and come down from the cross." Jesus looks down, with that same sad, loving look He gave me at the High Priest's house, and He says, "Father, forgive them for they do not know what they are doing." I suddenly realise that this forgiveness is meant for me, too. I've let Him down, but He still loves me and forgives me. Now I can try to forgive myself.

Jesus speaks to His beloved mother, Mary. He gives her into John's care, and asks John to treat her as his own mother. I feel that in some way she is also my mother, and somehow I shall make my peace with her.

For the first and last time Jesus cries out in real agony: "My God, my God, why have you forsaken me?" This is what my denial has done to Him. Just for a moment He actually feels cut off from His Father in heaven. I know how much He loves His Father, and to think that even for a split second He should be separated from His Father must have been the greatest pain of all. He can hardly breathe, but with a last effort He says the words, "It is finished." Then He just lets go of life and gives His spirit into His Father's hands.

There is a strange silence, as if the world is stunned at what has happened. The Roman centurion in charge of the execution has been watching Jesus closely all this time and he cries out, "Truly, this was the Son of God." And now the storm breaks.

13. JESUS IS TAKEN DOWN FROM THE CROSS

The chief priests want everything tidied away before the start of the Sabbath, so the three crucified men must be removed from their crosses. The soldiers now return to break the legs of those still alive, but Jesus is already dead.

Two well-dressed men are approaching. I recognise them as Joseph of Arimathea and Nicodemus, who were secret friends of Jesus. All the while they have stayed in the background. Now they have brought ointment and burial cloths, and Joseph offers his own tomb as a resting place for Jesus.

I can imagine how Mary must be feeling as Jesus is taken down from the cross and laid in her lap. Surely, there can be no sorrow like hers, yet, at the same time she feels immense gratitude for what Jesus has done. She never once doubted Him, even though she didn't always understand the things He told her. But now she just wants a little time to hold her Son in her arms and mourn for Him.

14. Jesus is buried

A sad and quiet little procession takes Jesus the short distance to the tomb where He will be buried. I feel so lost. I don't know what to do next: But now I remember a strange thing Jesus said to me shortly before He was arrested: "Peter, Satan has been given leave to test you, but I have prayed for you so that afterwards you will be stronger and be able to strengthen the others." Perhaps He wanted me, weak as I am to be a tower of strength and some sort of leader of His disciples. How could He have had such faith in me! I must go and find the others, and together we will wait and see what happens.

Conclusion

Lord Jesus, we thank you for allowing us to make this journey with you to Calvary accompanied by Peter. Like him, by our sins we have denied you many times, but we know you have forgiven us when we've said we are sorry. We look forward to the day of our resurrection when we shall be with you and Peter in heaven forever.

The Way of the Cross with John

INTRODUCTION

Heavenly Father, may we appreciate just how evil sin is. It was sin that took the most beautiful life that ever lived and nailed it to a cross. Let us now make the Way of the Cross in the company of John, the beloved disciple.

1. JESUS IS CONDEMNED TO DEATH

I am John. Because I've always been so close to Jesus, I am known as 'the beloved disciple'. Was it only last night we were all at supper together? And then in the Garden of Gethsemane Jesus prayed to His Father in such distress, while we fell asleep. "Couldn't you watch for one hour with me?" He said to us. He needed the company of His friends. Seeing Him now, I wish I had stayed awake. Judas the traitor has gone into hiding and I don't know where he and the others are, but I'll stay close to Jesus for as long as I can. Pilate is bringing Him out now, having condemned Him to the most cruel of deaths. The Pharisees and chief priests are gloating, having achieved exactly what they wanted: Jesus will die, but at the hands of the Romans.

2. JESUS RECEIVES HIS CROSS

They place the heavy cross on His shoulders and He takes their rough treatment so quietly and calmly. I remember Him saying to us, "You cannot be my disciple unless you take up your cross and follow Me," and now I see those words in action. He never asked us to do anything He wasn't prepared to do Himself. He takes up this dreadful burden on our behalf. How He must love us!

3.   JESUS FALLS THE FIRST TIME

Jesus falls to His knees, just as He did in Gethsemane in that hour of fear when He begged to be spared this agony. Perhaps He is thinking at this moment of all those people who began following Him so eagerly, but soon fell away, like the seed which fell on stony ground. How many of His followers could be called fair weather friends. They followed Him for what they could get for themselves and not for love of Him. His love for us spurs Him on to rise to His feet. With great dignity He continues the journey.

4.   JESUS MEETS HIS MOTHER

I'm glad that I have been able to accompany Mary on this journey. I hope I am bringing her some comfort. In this crowd there have been times when I have had to put my arm around her to protect her from being crushed. At these times I have sensed she has wanted to get near Jesus. At last there is an opportunity and she leaves me to reach Him. I follow her closely. I know how deep is the bond between Jesus and Mary, and how much they love each other, and I can see that just the touch of Mary's hand gives Him extra strength. She knows and understands that He is doing His Father's will, for there was nothing more important to Jesus than that, because He and the Father are one. The soldiers move Jesus along, and Mary comes back to me. Jesus gives me a look and I know He is thanking me for being at His mother's side. I treasure that look, but there is no need for Jesus to thank me, the privilege is mine.

5.   THE CROSS IS LAID UPON SIMON OF CYRENE

All the time I have wanted to help Jesus carry His heavy cross. But I know from the beginning that the soldiers wouldn't allow it. I want to prove my love for Him. Jesus' strength is failing. But before I can get anywhere near Him, a man at the front of the crowd is seized by the Roman soldiers and made to walk with Jesus, taking some of the weight of the cross. How gladly I'd have done this service! But this stranger has been chosen instead. I remember Jesus' words, "Whoever serves me will be honoured by my Father," and I'm sure that God will reward this man.

6.   VERONICA WIPES THE FACE OF JESUS

A woman appears as if from nowhere, walking bravely past the soldiers with a clean towel in her hand. I don't know who she is, but perhaps she once heard Jesus preach, or received some blessing from Him, and now she wants to repay Him with a kind gesture. She carefully wipes the blood and sweat from His face, and He blesses her again with His loving smile. As she removes the towel, the image of His dear face appears on it. People standing nearby are astonished, but it doesn't surprise me at all. I've seen many of His miracles, and I know His generosity so well.

7.   JESUS FALLS THE SECOND TIME

Two other men, both thieves, are to be crucified with Jesus today. The soldiers are urging all the prisoners to keep moving, but I can see how exhausted Jesus is, and He falls again. I can scarcely recognise my dear friend, bowed down under such terrible suffering. He once said to us, "The world must be shown that I love the Father." Surely, the world can see it now!

8.   THE WOMEN OF JERUSALEM MOURN FOR JESUS

Now Jesus is confronted by a group of local women, all weeping for Him. Some of them have their children with them. They know that Jesus loves them all. They experienced His love when He walked among them, blessing their children, healing their sick relatives, and just talking and listening to them. They are horrified now to see their friend being taken away to be crucified. He makes the effort to speak to them, telling them they should weep for themselves rather than for Him. No man could have greater love than this, to lay down His life for his friends.

9.   JESUS FALLS THE THIRD TIME

It causes me such anguish to see Jesus fall a third time; the Son of God on His knees in the dust and dirt. I know His thoughts so well, and I'm sure He is thinking of all those companions who followed Him faithfully until He was arrested. Where are they now? He seems to have so few friends left. We all loved Him, but fear or doubt made us desert Him at the last minute. It is our weakness which makes Him fall. Jesus makes one last gallant effort and gets to His feet, and completes the last few yards to the top of Calvary.

10. Jesus is stripped of His garments

Jesus, our gentle and loving Master, is cruelly seized by the soldiers. They pull His clothes from His back, re-opening His wounds, and it's a shock to see the terrible lacerations caused by that brutal scourging. Mary gasps, and I put my arm around her to comfort her. I remember Jesus saying, "If a man asks you for your shirt, give him your coat also." And here is Jesus giving away everything He possesses.

11. Jesus is nailed to the cross

The soldiers offer all the condemned men some drugged wine to deaden their pain, but Jesus refuses it. I know He wants to share every possible human suffering. No one will ever be able to say that Jesus doesn't understand.

The soldiers pull Jesus to the ground and lie Him on His cross. Jesus stretches out His arms on the cross, offering His hands to be nailed. The sound of the hammer sends a shudder through my body. Mary immediately bows her head and blocks her ears and I put my arms around her. I can feel Mary's pain, too; each nail must be like a sword piercing her heart.

The three crosses are erected, Jesus in the middle between the two thieves. Above His head there is a sign in three languages telling the world that He is Jesus of Nazareth, King of the Jews. I remember that He once said to us, "When I am lifted up I shall draw all mankind to me." Will the world recognise Him now? Some of the onlookers start calling out, "Let Him come down off the cross, if He is really the Messiah." How could they speak to Jesus like that! Yet, Jesus loves them so much He prays that His Father will forgive them.

12. JESUS DIES ON THE CROSS

It's the hottest hour of the day, and still Jesus hangs on His cross, in the utmost agony. No wonder He is thirsty. Someone brings a sponge soaked in vinegar and puts it to His lips. He told us at our last supper that He would never drink wine again until He drinks the new wine in His Father's kingdom. I'm still not sure exactly what that means, but I do know that what He really thirsts for is our friendship, our love.

The sky begins to darken, as if nature itself is appalled at what is happening. Jesus looks lovingly at His mother and at me. "Woman, behold your son," He says to Mary. "Behold your mother," He tells me, giving His beloved mother into my care. Mary looks gratefully at me and I know that from now on she will have a home with me.

Jesus cries aloud, "It is finished." All that He came into the world to do is now accomplished and He can give back His spirit to His Father in heaven. I'm trying to be strong, for Mary's sake, but it's Mary who turns to comfort me, giving me the love she gave to Jesus.

13. JESUS IS TAKEN DOWN FROM THE CROSS

The Jewish priests are anxious to have the bodies removed before the Sabbath, so now the soldiers finish their task. The two thieves have their legs broken, but Jesus is already dead. Nevertheless, one soldier vindictively stabs his lance into Jesus' side and blood and water pours out. In doing this the Scripture is fulfiled, 'Not one of His bones shall be broken'.

Two wealthy men arrive, Nicodemus and Joseph of Arimathea, who have secretly been good friends of Jesus. We are allowed to take His body down from the cross, and Mary cradles her Son in her arms, as she must have done so many times when He was young. These two men have brought costly ointment of myrrh and aloes and a fine linen cloth in which to wrap Jesus' body, and so we prepare Him for burial.

14. JESUS IS BURIED

Joseph has a new tomb, built for his own use, in a garden not far from here. He offers it to Mary as a burial place for Jesus, and she appreciates his kindness. This brings to mind something Jesus once said: "Foxes have holes, and the birds of the air have their nests, but the Son of Man has nowhere to lay his head." But now He has a grave in which to rest, thanks to the generosity of a rich man.

It's a very small group, the last of His faithful friends, who accompany Jesus to His resting place. As the stone is rolled across the entrance to the tomb I wonder whether this is really the end of the story.

CONCLUSION

Jesus, John loved to be known as your beloved disciple, for so he was. We know you have no favourites and that you love us all equally. But does our love for you match the love that John had for you? Enable us to love you as he did. We thank you for allowing us to have accompanied you on this journey.

The Way of the Cross
with Mary Magdalene

INTRODUCTION

Today we are making the Stations of the Cross side by side with Mary Magdalene. She was a woman who became a prostitute and found herself trapped in that sinful way of life. The turning point in her life was her meeting with Jesus. He showed her that no matter how low she had fallen it was possible for her to repent and be released from sin. Mary was privileged to hear from Jesus' own lips those wonderful words, "Your sins are forgiven." Her life was transformed, and in love and gratitude she became one of Jesus' most devoted friends.

1.   JESUS IS CONDEMNED TO DEATH

I am Mary of Magdala. I know that Jesus is my Saviour, and that He is laying down His life for all of us sinners. I love Him so much, and wish that everyone could love Him as I do, but here in this crowd there are people who hate and despise Him, and they are shouting, "Crucify Him!" If only they knew who He really is! At this moment Pilate is at his seat of judgement. The soldiers bring Jesus back to Pilate. What they have done to my Lord? They've plaited a crown of thorns and placed it on His head. I can see the blood stains on His clothing from the scourging. It's an effort for Jesus to stand upright. How can anyone be so brutal to my Lord? Even Pilate is shocked at His appearance. He is hoping that His accusers will now be satisfied at the punishment He has received and let Him go free. But they shout even louder, "Crucify Him! Crucify Him!" Pilate repeats, "I can find no fault in this man." Realising that they are determined to kill Jesus, he says, "Take Him and crucify Him yourselves." Calling for some water he washes his hands of the whole affair." Priests and people cry out, "His blood be upon us and upon our children." I can't believe this travesty of justice! How could they treat my Lord in this way? And so poor Jesus is condemned to death.

2. JESUS RECEIVES HIS CROSS

I can see the soldiers placing the heavy cross on Jesus' shoulder. He accepts it calmly and purposefully, because He loves us and knows that this cross will free us from sin. I know only too well that it is the weight of my sin which He now has to bear, and I think with shame of the sins of my past life. When I was a young girl I was headstrong and impulsive. I wanted what I thought were the good things of life. I got into bad company and soon found myself earning my living from prostitution. It was Jesus who made me realise that it was possible to live a better life. I know I can never repay Him for what He has done and is doing for me. Two other men are being crucified along with Jesus. I hear that they are both thieves, and I pray that they, too, will be given the chance to repent and be forgiven.

3. JESUS FALLS THE FIRST TIME

Jesus has hardly begun His painful journey, but He is already struggling under His burden. He falls down on the stony road and I see a frown of pain on His face, but He does not cry out. The cross seems almost too heavy for Him to lift. I remember how weighed down I felt during those years of degradation when I worked as a prostitute. I hated the men who exploited me and treated me as an object for their use. I hated myself for allowing them to use me in that way. I felt worthless and dirty, yet although my conscience troubled me I was trapped in a habit of life which I could not break. Then one day I heard Jesus preaching. He spoke of repentance, and He made me see that it was possible even for me to be forgiven. With His help I knew I could change my life and He lifted me with hope. Now Jesus summons the strength to get to His feet again. I pray for all those who become involved in prostitution, that with Jesus' help they will find the strength to change their lives.

4.   Jesus meets His sorrowful mother

Mary, the mother of Jesus, is accompanying her Son on this journey, hoping for an opportunity to speak to Him. Now she makes her way through the crowd and He pauses to greet her with His loving smile. As their hands touch, they seem to be reassuring each other. I wish I could be close to Jesus just once more, but this is Mary's special moment. I know she loves Him dearly. She is so distressed at her Son's pitiful condition, but at the same time she's proud of Him. My mother was ashamed of me because of the life I led, but if she could see me today she would be so thankful for God's mercy. I would like to comfort all mothers whose children have brought them heartache and disgrace. I know that there is always hope.

5.   The cross is laid upon Simon of Cyrene

Jesus looks completely exhausted. His face is pale. His shoulders and hands are bleeding from the constant friction of the cross. His feet are sore and dirty, and I can see that each step is a tremendous effort. He stops, as if He is about to faint, and the soldiers are afraid that He won't be able to carry His own cross any further. How I would love to help Him, but who would pay any attention to me, a mere woman? Now a man in the crowd has been brought forward by the soldiers and they bully him into taking up Jesus' cross. He resists at first, but I can see that he is struck by the goodness of Jesus, just as I was. He soon changes his attitude and gladly accepts the task he's been given. What an honour it is to be able to help Jesus!

6.   Veronica wipes the face of Jesus

The prisoners move on, and a local woman now comes out of her house and approaches Jesus, carrying a clean cloth with which to bathe His face. She takes pity on Him, seeing how bravely He bears His suffering. Gently, she wipes away the dirt, sweat and blood, bringing Him some relief. This woman reminds me of my first meeting with Jesus. His preaching had touched me deeply. All I wanted was to meet Him personally. Hearing that He was dining at the home of Simon the Pharisee, I made up my mind to go there and see Him. I took with me the most expensive ointment of myrrh I could buy, and somehow I found the courage to approach Jesus. I knelt at His feet and began to anoint them. In His presence I felt so unworthy and so conscious of my sins, that I wept with remorse, wetting His feet with my tears and wiping them with my hair. Jesus rewarded me that day, and He now rewards this kind woman with a grateful smile. As she removes her cloth and begins to fold it up she finds on it the image of His beloved face, a permanent remembrance of their meeting. I feel sure that her life will be changed now, as mine was.

7. JESUS FALLS THE SECOND TIME

Jesus is very weak now, and He stumbles and falls a second time. I feel the shock of that fall, and I weep at the thought of the pain He must be enduring. As I see my dear Lord on His knees I think again of that day when I met Him in Simon's house. I had fallen so low in sin, and my reputation was known to everyone. There were gasps of horror from the guests, when they saw me kneeling at Jesus' feet. I could see Simon glaring at me in disgust, knowing what I was, but I shall never forget the kind words of Jesus, "Your sins are forgiven. Your faith has saved you. Go in peace." He restored my self respect and lifted my spirits that day. Now I see Jesus summoning His strength to get to His feet again.

8. JESUS MEETS THE WOMEN OF JERUSALEM

Soon after this we encounter some women who on seeing Jesus openly weep in sympathy for Him. Like me I am sure they too could relate how they had in some way experienced the goodness of Jesus. In fact, while on my travels with Jesus, I can recognise some of the women. For the last few months I, along with my privileged friends Joanna and Susanna, have been helping Jesus and His apostles in their work. I've loved this work for it has kept me close to Jesus, my Lord, and has given me an opportunity to show my gratitude to Him and make up for the wrongness of my past life. The centurion gives Jesus the chance to pause for a while and speak to the women. I can see that Jesus is grateful for their concern. Without thought for Himself, He warns them of the danger that lies in the future for themselves and their children. They look puzzled but before they can ask any questions the centurion gives the command for the prisoners to move on.

9. JESUS FALLS THE THIRD TIME

The hill of Calvary is in sight. I'm glad my Lord hasn't very far to go. I can see the blood appearing on His garment above His shoulder. He must be feeling the pain from that wound. He falls again. He must be very weak. These next few yards are going to be extremely hard for Him, but I know no matter how tired and exhausted He is, He will complete this journey. His determination inspires me to persevere to the end. Jesus rescued me from a sinful life and I never, never want to fall again.

10. JESUS IS STRIPPED OF HIS GARMENTS

The soldiers take the cross from Jesus' shoulder and for a moment He looks relieved. Immediately they roughly drag His robe off His back. Jesus winces in pain as His wounds are reopened. There He now stands naked before us all. Jesus, forgive me for the many times I have been unchaste. It is my sins that have brought you to this.

11. JESUS IS NAILED TO THE CROSS

This is something I don't know how I'm going to face. How can any man nail another to a cross? It's barbaric! I love Jesus, my Lord, so much. How must Mary, His mother be feeling, who loves Him so much more? The thieves protest at being fastened to their crosses, but Jesus doesn't resist. Jesus has to be the bravest man this world has ever known, for no one has loved as He loves. I've known many men in my life, but not one of them has ever loved me as this man Jesus, my Lord. I can now hear the hammering of the nails and I want it to finish. When are they going to stop? At last the hammering is over and the crosses are erected. Some of the onlookers cheer.

12. JESUS DIES ON THE CROSS

As Jesus hangs on His cross I can now move close to Him. I caress and kiss His bleeding feet. Someone in the crowd calls out to Jesus to come down from the cross and prove that He is the Messiah and they will believe in Him. Why can't they see that He is the Messiah?

I feel for Jesus as He is having difficulty breathing. I can hear His rasping breath. He is not going to be left to die in peace. Even one of the criminals is cursing Him and telling Him to use His power and release them all if He is the Messiah. I'm glad the other thief is defending Jesus. Not only does He do that, but He is given the faith to ask for a place in His kingdom. Jesus promises him that his request will be granted today. How I'd love to be with Jesus in His kingdom, today!

As the hours pass by the sky darkens and the air is oppressive. Even the soldiers who are throwing their dice have difficulty seeing and are aware of something strange going on. Heavenly Father, I never thought the time would come when I would want to see Jesus taken from me. But I ask you to take His life and end His sufferings now. I can't bear to see Him lingering on in such agony. I think my prayer is being answered for Jesus says, "It is finished," and He commends Himself to His Father. And with that He dies. Immediately, the centurion who has been watching and listening intently to all that has been going on, proclaims, "Indeed, He is a Holy Man! He is the Son of God." Another man has come to believe in the goodness of Jesus!

13. Jesus is taken down from the cross

I now leave my position at the cross and I want to console Mary. I put my arms round her to let her know that I feel for her. Two of Jesus' friends have arrived to take His body down from the cross. I see that Nicodemus has a jar of ointment of myrrh and aloes. I recall the words Jesus spoke to His disciples when they complained about me anointing His feet with a jar of precious ointment, "Leave her alone. She has come beforehand to anoint my body for burial." I know Mary will allow me to help her to do this last act of kindness to Jesus, her Son. We can now set about preparing Jesus' body for burial and we generously anoint it. We have to hurry for time is short and the Sabbath is about to begin.

14. Jesus is laid in the sepulchre

Mary accepts Joseph's kind offer to bury her Son in his own tomb. Joseph, Nicodemus and John reverently carry Jesus' body to the tomb in a nearby garden. They place Jesus' body on the cold slab in the tomb. The men leave the tomb and wait outside allowing us women to spend a little time to grieve with Jesus. My prayer to Jesus is, "With you Jesus, I bury my sins." We leave the tomb and the three men roll the heavy stone against its entrance. Already I've made up my mind that as soon as the Sabbath is over I'll be back to complete the anointing. With a heavy heart we return to our homes.

CONCLUSION.

Jesus said, "There is more rejoicing in heaven over one sinner who repents than over ninety nine who have no need of repentance." How true those words are in the case of His dear friend Mary Magdalene.

She was once a great sinner but now we venerate her as a great saint. This should give all of us hope. The gospels record that she was the first one to witness the Risen Lord. That has to tell us something about her greatness and how much Jesus loved her.

Let us conclude by recalling another saying of Jesus on her behalf when she anointed His body while still alive, "I tell you this: wherever in all the world the gospel is proclaimed, what she has done will be told as her memorial".

The Way of the Cross with Longinus, the Centurion

1. JESUS IS CONDEMNED TO DEATH

I am Longinus, the Roman centurion. We have three men to crucify today, and I'm in charge of the execution squad. Who is this man Jesus, and why is there such a fuss about Him? From what I hear, He hasn't committed any crime, but the crowd are yelling for His blood. Always squabbling about something, these Jews. If Pilate didn't hand Him over there would be a riot, and so to keep the peace He must have allowed this man to be crucified. Why should an innocent man be executed? Well, I have my job to do so I just obey orders.

2. JESUS RECEIVES HIS CROSS

There's something different about this Jesus. I've seen a good many crucifixions, and most of the criminals protest and struggle and swear at us. But this man is calm and dignified. He smiles at me and He takes the cross on his shoulder so willingly, He almost seems glad to be given it. I don't understand the man.

3. JESUS FALLS THE FIRST TIME

They usually have trouble carrying their cross. After all, it weighs around 16 stone, the weight of a well-built soldier in full armour, so I'm not surprised that Jesus is on His knees. One of my men drags Him to His feet and Jesus looks at him and says thank you. I admire this man's courage, and He's still a puzzle to me.

4. JESUS MEETS HIS MOTHER

A Jewish woman pushes through the crowd, saying she is the mother of Jesus. It must be hard for her, seeing her son in this situation. The world stops as they look at each other. Even though her heart aches as she sees her Son suffer so dreadfully, she seems to be encouraging Him to carry on. I can see by the way they are looking at each other that this is no ordinary mother and son relationship. I am beginning to see that Jesus' death is for some purpose. He is sacrificing Himself and His mother is a part of it. I can relate to that for we Romans know what it is to die for honour.

5. THE CROSS IS LAID UPON SIMON OF CYRENE

Progress is slow. Jesus is dragging His feet, and we need to get this execution over and done with before the Sabbath starts. I notice a tall, strong looking man who has been following us for some time, mingling with the crowd of onlookers. I signal to my men and they drag him forward and make him take one end of the wooden cross. He's reluctant at first, but Jesus turns and looks at him gratefully, and then, to my surprise, he seems quite glad to be able to help.

6. VERONICA WIPES THE FACE OF JESUS

A woman comes out of a nearby house carrying a towel. Without any fear of my soldiers she goes straight to Jesus and gently places the towel against His face. This brings Him some relief. Then, an amazing thing happens. On removing her towel, she finds on it an image of Jesus' face. It's some kind of miracle—who is this man?

7. JESUS FALLS THE SECOND TIME

I can't help feeling sorry for Jesus. He's having a hard time, and it is not as if He is guilty like the other two. He falls heavily, cutting His knees on the stony road, but some how finds the strength to get up again. What makes Him do it? How can He carry on, knowing all the time that He is innocent?

8. JESUS MEETS THE WOMEN OF JERUSALEM

We are delayed again, this time by a group of .Jewish women weeping over Jesus. How do they know this man? Why do they have such feeling for Him? There must be something special about Him – they don't show any interest in the two thieves. My men want to push the women aside but I hold my hand up to allow Him to speak to them. He talks to them, saying that they should weep for themselves and for Jerusalem. Is He some sort of prophet, I wonder?

9. JESUS FALLS THE THIRD TIME

We are within sight of the hilltop and Jesus falls again. The two thieves are whimpering now, but still not one word of complaint or protest comes from Jesus' lips. Although He is physically weaker, mentally He is more determined to see the whole thing through. There's something holy about this man that almost frightens me.

10. JESUS IS STRIPPED OF HIS GARMENTS

My men begin to remove the garments of the criminals. They work quickly and efficiently causing Jesus some pain. He still doesn't complain. One of the perks of our job is being allowed to claim the criminals' clothes. Usually we divide everything, but Jesus' robe is of such good quality, it seems a pity to cut the cloth, so we decide to cast lots for it.

11. JESUS IS NAILED TO THE CROSS

I offer all the condemned men some drugged wine. Jesus thanks me but shakes His head. He doesn't want to be spared any of the pain. We've been ordered to fasten a sign on Jesus' cross saying, 'Jesus of Nazareth, the King of the Jews'. Perhaps that's who He is, a holy man and a king. There is something regal about Him even in this condition. Though He is naked, I am the one who feels uneasy. I am a hardened soldier, I have witnessed this many times, but I can see the goodness in this man. If I didn't have my job to do I'd let Him go free. But It Is too late now, already my men are hammering the nails through His wrists. I know He must be in agony, but He holds back any scream.

12. JESUS DIES ON THE CROSS

There is a strange atmosphere, the air is heavy, a storm is brewing. It's not yet three o'clock and already it getting dark. I have to stay till the end to make sure the crucifixion is properly carried out. During the last three hours Jesus hasn't been able to speak much, but what He said has opened my eyes. One of the thieves started sneering at Him, saying "Are you the Messiah? Why don't you save us and yourself?" But the other thief said, "We deserve to die because we are guilty. This man has done nothing wrong. Jesus remember me when you come into your kingdom." Jesus looked at him lovingly as He said, "I promise you this very day you will be with me in paradise". How could He make such a promise unless He was able to keep it. We have nailed Jesus to this cross, but in some way He is in control. He is making it so clear that he is willingly going to his death. His life is not being taken from him. At last He cries out, "It is finished." His job is done—and so is ours. I feel ashamed now and in front of everyone I have to say out loud, "This was an innocent and holy man."

13. JESUS IS TAKEN DOWN FROM THE CROSS

Two well-to-do men, one of them a Pharisee, have been given permission to take Jesus' body down from the cross. I can't help but notice how they treat Jesus. They are so gentle and my soldiers were so rough. They lay Him in the arms of His mother who's been supporting Him all through the journey. How tenderly she removes the crown of thorns and gently touches the wounds in His hands and side. Jesus knows that this was not a useless shameful death, but some kind of triumph and she has been a part of it.

14. JESUS IS LAID IN THE SEPULCHRE

I was summoned to give my report. Pilate was surprised at how quickly Jesus had died, but he gave permission for His body to be taken away for burial. Jesus' friends are now carrying His body to a tomb carved out of the rock and a large stone is rolled across the entrance. The Pharisees have asked for a guard to watch the tomb because Jesus promised to rise from the dead on the third day. Something tells me that He will keep His promise. I shall wait and see.

CONCLUSION

Jesus, we thank you for allowing us to accompany you on this journey. As we make our way through life, let us never forget what you did for us. May our lives be worthy of your death, and may all of us rise in glory with you on the last day.

The Way of the Cross with Dismas, the 'Good Thief'

INTRODUCTION

Jesus, have we the courage to die with you? Dismas, the Good Thief was given this privilege, we will now make this journey with you through the eyes of Dismas.

1. JESUS IS CONDEMNED TO DEATH

They call me Dismas. I've been on the wrong side of the law most of my life, and now the law has caught up with me. I've been given the death penalty, the punishment for theft, along with another thief and a man called Jesus. I don't know why He's here with us. I heard Pilate, the Roman governor, say that He didn't deserve to die and should be let off with a flogging, but the crowd is shouting, "Crucify him! Give us Barabbas!" So Barabbas, a man charged with murder, walks free, while this man Jesus is condemned to death.

2. JESUS RECEIVES HIS CROSS

The Roman soldiers have no sympathy for any of us. We are roughly handled, and then we are each given our own cross to carry. It's terribly heavy, and already splinters are pricking my hands. I have to carry this hateful thing all the way up the hill, knowing that when I get to the top the soldiers will fasten me to it. Jesus takes His cross up quietly without complaining. You'd almost think He was doing this willingly. I know why I and the other criminal have been sentenced – we're thieves – but why is He here? Ah! I can see the standard bearer carrying the sign to indicate His crime. It reads, 'Jesus of Nazareth, the King of the Jews'. Can He really be a king? Is that why He is wearing this crown of thorns?

3. JESUS FALLS THE FIRST TIME

My hands are sore and there is a burning pain in my shoulder. I hate this cross, and I can hear the other thief groaning and cursing too. Jesus says nothing, but He is obviously suffering. His clothes are soaked with sweat and I can see the marks of the flogging across His back and shoulders. He falls down and I notice streaks of blood on His face as the thorns dig deeper into His forehead. If I were Jesus I would have pulled off that crown by now, but He seems almost proud to be wearing it. A strange kingdom where the king allows Himself to be treated like this!

4. JESUS MEETS HIS MOTHER

A woman breaks through the crowd just in front of Jesus. I wonder who she can be? Then I hear someone in the crowd saying, "There's Mary, His mother." I think of my own mother, who loved me so much. What hopes she had for me! And I've let her down. "Ah! Mum, I'm sorry!," I'm glad you can't see me now, disgraced like this. I wouldn't be able to face you. Jesus and His mother look at each other and I can see there is a special bond between them. She must believe He is innocent yet she seems to be encouraging Him to go on. He looks at her reassuringly. Perhaps He is hoping for a last minute reprieve.

5. SIMON OF CYRENE HELPS JESUS TO CARRY THE CROSS

Jesus is really struggling now. It is so much worse for Him. He had that terrible Roman scourging. At least we were spared that. The soldiers are trying to hurry us along, so they pick on a man in the crowd and make him help to carry Jesus' cross. Of course, he's reluctant. But Jesus gives him a grateful look and a change comes over him. Now he shoulders the cross as if it's a privilege. What does he see in Jesus?

6. VERONICA WIPES THE FACE OF JESUS

The heat is intense and we all feel sick and dizzy. A woman boldly steps in front of the soldiers and goes to Jesus, gently dabbing His face with a damp cloth. I almost envy Him. I long for the relief of cool water on my face. Jesus smiles at the woman and thanks her for her kindness. Then she discovers that the cloth she used has the image of Jesus' face on it. I can see it quite clearly and I wonder again who this Jesus really is. Everyone He touches is changed somehow. Perhaps He could have changed me, but it is too late now.

7. JESUS FALLS THE SECOND TIME

We are half way through the journey. I wonder how I would have coped if Jesus had not been with us. He is so calm and brave. I can feel some of His strength. I know if He wasn't here all my thoughts would be centred on myself. But I keep watching Him and seeing how He is coping. Even with help, Jesus finds it difficult and He falls again, but with great determination He gets up and moves forward. Where does He find the strength? How can He accept this punishment when He isn't guilty?

8. JESUS MEETS THE WOMEN OF JERUSALEM

A group of women at the roadside start crying noisily when they see Jesus approaching. What makes them cry over Him? No one cries for us and we're suffering the same fate. He pauses as if He has something important to say to them. "Don't weep for me," He says, "but for yourselves and for your children." All I can feel is my own pain, but here is Jesus feeling sorry for other people. There's something in Him that is quite unlike ordinary men.

9. JESUS FALLS THE THIRD TIME

I am totally exhausted and wracked with pain and Jesus must be feeling exactly the same. We've almost reached Golgotha, that terrible place where we are to be crucified. I am shaking with fear, but look at Jesus after falling the third time He is on His feet again and walking deliberately, willingly towards death. How I wish I had some of His courage!

10. JESUS IS STRIPPED OF HIS GARMENTS

The soldiers strip us of our clothes, exposing us to the jeering crowd. One more painful blow, one more humiliation. We can see now the holes in the ground where the crosses will be erected and the sight makes me tremble even more. Jesus bears it all so calmly and patiently. Whatever He has done He doesn't deserve to die, yet He's facing death with no trace of fear and not one harsh word for His executioners. I know, if He is a real man, He must be trembling too, but He doesn't show it.

11. JESUS IS NAILED TO THE CROSS

This is the worst of all – held down by the soldiers and fastened to the cross. I cry out with terror and I can hear the other thief screaming too. They are hammering nails into Jesus' wrists now, but no cry comes from Him. The three crosses are raised up and the pain to my arms and chest almost makes me faint. Jesus is in the middle with a sign fixed to His cross saying, 'Jesus of Nazareth, the king of the Jews'. Passers by start mocking Him and telling Him to come down from the cross, if He really is a king. He actually prays for them: "Father forgive them for they do not know what they are doing."

12. JESUS DIES ON THE CROSS

The pain is unbearable now. Jesus whispers "I'm thirsty," but all He gets is a sponge soaked in vinegar. The other thief complains bitterly to Jesus. "If you are the Messiah why don't you save yourself and us?". "Aren't you ashamed," I say to him sharply, "We are guilty and deserve to be punished. This man Jesus has done nothing wrong, yet He is suffering exactly as we are." I'm beginning to understand that Jesus is not being robbed of His life, He's giving it away. He's no longer a prisoner because no one has power over Him. Is it too late for me to tell Him I believe in Him? I call out to Him, "Jesus, remember me when you come into your kingdom." He turns His face towards me, slowly and painfully. He says nothing about the life I have led, the crimes I've committed. He just says, "My friend, I promise you this very day you will be with me in paradise." With a last prayer He gives Himself into His Father's hands and dies. I'm so glad that I was given the time to speak to Him. Now I understand how He has touched so many lives and I can appreciate why Simon thought it a privilege to help carry His cross.

13. JESUS IS TAKEN DOWN FROM THE CROSS

My own death is very close now. I can see the soldiers coming to finish us off by breaking our legs. But I am not afraid any more, because Jesus has promised me a place in His kingdom. When they come to Jesus they find He's already dead and cruelly pierce His side with a lance. A soldier comes towards me and with a hammer is about to break my legs. With that our story teller dies. It is now up to us to continue the story. Jesus' mother and His friends, who have been standing by His cross all this time, now take His body down. Mary rocks Him in her arms as she must have done many times when He was a child. How sad this loving mother is, but how glad she must be that her Son is entering His kingdom.

14. JESUS IS LAID IN THE SEPULCHRE

A wealthy man comes to take charge of Jesus. His body is wrapped in a fine cloth and taken away for burial in a newly built tomb. Jesus, I thank you for the generous way you died for us. I am sure there was no need for you to go to such lengths of suffering. Not one of us can ever complain and say you could have loved us more. It is you who could make that complaint about us. Like Dismas, the Good Thief may we all be given the time to repent and not have the fate of a sudden and unprovided death.

In the footsteps of Jesus and Simon of Cyrene

INTRODUCTION

Today we consider the part played by Simon of Cyrene on Jesus' road to Calvary. Simon was an outsider, a mere onlooker who had no intention of becoming involved. Yet, it was Simon who exemplified the words of Jesus, "If anyone wants to be a follower of mine, let him renounce himself and take up his cross every day and follow me". In these stations we are going to see that each person we meet accepts or rejects their own cross.

Take the cross you are given, come and follow me. I will lead you to heaven If you follow me. If you follow me.

1. JESUS IS CONDEMNED TO DEATH

We know that Simon was originally from the town of Cyrene in Libya, but had settled in the countryside outside Jerusalem with his wife and two sons, Alexander and Rufus. On this Friday morning he came into the city, on business. As he is travelling into Jerusalem Jesus is being presented to the furious mob who want to see Him die.

It was Caiaphas and Pilate who condemned Jesus to death on the cross. Their cross was to admit the truth and see that justice should be done, but they refused to accept it. Caiaphas could have acknowledged Jesus as the Messiah, but he was too stubborn to take up the cross of humility. Pilate could have let Jesus go free, since he believed he was innocent, but he could not face the prospect of losing Caesar's favour and thereby losing his position.

When we try to avoid difficult decisions or take the easy way out we are rejecting our cross. Experience should teach us that when we do this we are only making ourselves carry a heavier cross. Pilate rejected his, but then he had the heavier cross to carry, namely that of a guilty conscience which he had to live with till the day he died.

2.   Jesus receives His cross

At this point Simon appears on the scene. He notices the crowd gathering outside the Governor's palace and he is naturally drawn towards it, out of curiosity. He feels pity for the three men he sees being given their heavy crosses to carry. The one he pities most is the one who is wearing that painful crown of thorns, which has already drawn streaks of blood from His forehead. He can see from His bloodstained garments that He has already been severely punished by scourging. Simon wonders who this man is and he is impressed by the calm, dignified manner in which He accepts His cross.

We know that Jesus was glad to take up the cross, because it was the means of our salvation.

Jesus, by His example, is teaching us how we are to bear hard and distasteful crosses in our own lives; and to use every cross for a good purpose. No cross should ever be wasted.

3.   Jesus falls the first time

Simon senses that there is something unusual about Jesus and he finds himself mesmerised and irresistibly drawn to follow Him. Almost without realising it, he finds himself following the procession. He watches Jesus intently and sees that He is walking very slowly and painfully as He drags the cross along. Suddenly, He trips and falls and the heavy cross falls with Him, causing Him more pain and bruising. Yet, He gets to His feet again after a few moments and carries on. Simon can't help admiring the courage of Jesus and His quiet determination. Unlike the other two prisoners, He seems to have a sense of purpose. The other two appear angry and disgruntled, occasionally shouting curses at the soldiers.

Jesus as a man experienced physical pain and suffering just as we do. He felt our weakness, but He knew that His Father would give Him the strength to carry His cross.

God is our loving Father and it would be unthinkable that He should give us a cross that we cannot bear. He gives us strength to cope with all our difficulties and overcome our weakness. We also have Jesus our brother to help us. When we feel unequal to the task let us remember His words, "I am with you always."

4. JESUS MEETS HIS AFFLICTED MOTHER

Simon is surprised to see a woman approaching Jesus. She goes up to Jesus and touches His arm, and He turns to look at her. There is such deep feeling in that look, and Simon realises that the woman must be Jesus' mother. No words are spoken, for none are necessary. Simon can see the love and understanding which this mother and son share, and the comfort they are able to give each other. They have only a few moments together, and then Simon hears the soldiers shouting to all the prisoners to move on.

Our Lady had her own cross to carry. She had to suffer the anguish of seeing her beloved Son tortured and crucified. What enabled her to bear this cross was her complete trust in God and her determination to do His will.

Sometimes we may have to bear the cross of seeing a loved one suffer and die. We can always approach our loving mother to help us accept our cross because she has walked this painful road before us and she understands the ache that is in our hearts.

5. THE CROSS IS LAID UPON SIMON OF CYRENE

Jesus is now struggling to put one foot in front of the other. Simon feels sorry for Him, seeing Him looking so pale and drained of energy. He can see that He is almost ready to collapse. The soldiers are impatient, because it looks as if Jesus will not be able to go any further without help. The procession halts while they decide what to do. The centurion on horseback points in Simon's direction and shouts to his men, "That strong-looking chap over there – he'll do!" Suddenly two soldiers come towards him, and Simon realises with horror that he's the one they want. "Why me?" he cries, as one of the soldiers takes him by the arm. "It's nothing to do with me. I don't want to get involved." The soldiers ignore his protests and push Simon forward to where Jesus stands, now almost leaning on His cross. Simon is afraid, and resentful. Then Jesus turns to look at him, with such a kind, loving smile, and touches Simon's arm in gratitude. Something happens at this moment, for in Jesus' touch there is the power to change Simon's heart. He feels the goodness and holiness that is in Jesus. His resentment vanishes, and he finds himself taking up the end of Jesus' cross and placing it on his own shoulder. At a command from the centurion, the procession moves on again, and Simon knows that there is now a bond of sympathy between himself and Jesus. He feels privileged to have been chosen to help.

Simon never wanted to carry the cross. Given the choice, he would have avoided it. When it was imposed upon him he accepted it grudgingly, but with Jesus' help he was able to change his attitude and see the value of the cross.

Simon helped Jesus to carry His cross and Jesus helped Simon to carry his. They were in it together. This is how we should treat a heavy cross that is placed on our shoulders. We're not alone. Jesus is our Simon and He can help us. We, too, can help Jesus. St. Paul indicates this when he writes, "Make up in your lives what is lacking in the sufferings of Christ." What a privilege is ours!

6. Veronica wipes the face of Jesus

As the procession moves slowly along the dusty road Simon feels sticky and thirsty. He knows how much worse Jesus must be feeling, having suffered so much already. The other two prisoners groan and curse, but Jesus makes no complaint. A woman steps out in front of the procession and walks straight up to Jesus. She carries a clean cloth dipped in cool water and immediately wipes Jesus' face, bathing away the sweat and dirt. Simon sees the refreshment she gives to Jesus and the thanks she receives. She is rewarded for there on the cloth is the image of Jesus' face. Simon is astonished and wonders again just who Jesus is.

Veronica's cross was to find the courage to face those Roman soldiers, and to take the trouble of bathing Jesus' face to bring Him some relief. In her own way she helped Jesus to carry His cross, for she lightened His burden.

Veronica was an opportunist. She saw Jesus in need of a little comfort and came to His help. She knew the soldiers would be an obstacle in reaching Jesus, but she did what needed doing. Are we like Veronica? We see many in need who have a cross to carry. There are obstacles to be overcome. Despite them, have we the courage to help like Veronica? If we do, Jesus will see that we don't go unrewarded.

7. JESUS FALLS THE SECOND TIME

Simon feels Jesus tiring again. His steps are faltering, He is breathing heavily, and suddenly He falls to the ground, bringing Simon down with Him. There is a moment of complete confusion. Simon scrambles to his feet and goes to help Jesus. Wincing with pain, Jesus gets up and nods to Simon to indicate that He is ready to go on.

In this fall Jesus must have experienced discouragement and frustration. Yet, He would not allow Himself to give up. With confidence in His Father's love and help, He was able to continue.

Jesus understands how discouraged we can be when we fail to make progress, or when we feel defeated by our problems. He wants us to know that we can always turn to Him, for He says, "Come to me, all you who labour and are overburdened, and I will give you rest."

8. JESUS MEETS THE WOMEN OF JERUSALEM

The journey is interrupted again as a group of local women arrive. They call out to Jesus and weep to see Him in such distress. Simon can see the great love these women have for Jesus, and also the love and concern He has for them. He tells them not to weep for Him; they will have cause to weep for themselves and their children's future. Simon listens in amazement as Jesus speaks of the troubles and disasters which are to come to Jerusalem. Is Jesus some kind of prophet, he wonders?

The women of Jerusalem could not accept the fact that Jesus, their friend, was being taken away from them. Neither could they understand when He tried to warn them about the cross they would have to bear in the future.

Our future is uncertain. We don't know what cross lies ahead of us. All we can do is to put our trust in our loving Father who will always give us grace to carry it. We have St. Paul to confirm this for when the cross lay heavily on him God told him, "My grace is sufficient for you."

9. JESUS FALLS THE THIRD TIME

Jesus is nearing the end of the journey and Simon notices that He is faltering again. He tries to take a little more of the weight of the cross, but Jesus is now so exhausted that even with Simon's help He cannot stay on His feet any longer. He falls, and lies on the ground for a while without moving. Simon goes to Him, thinking He has lost consciousness. At last, with great perseverance, and Simon's helping hand, Jesus manages to stand once more. Simon sees that they have almost reached Calvary, and he feels Jesus bracing Himself for one last effort.

How desperately tired Jesus must have felt at this last fall. He must have felt all the despair of those who find that they cannot carry their burden any further. He was sustained by His sense of purpose and the thought of the goal He was reaching.

When we have lost the will to carry on, let us remember Jesus' desperate effort to reach Calvary. He overcame fatigue and intense suffering. Nothing was to prevent Him from completing His mission. Jesus encourages us to do the same when He says, "He who perseveres to the end he will be saved."

10. JESUS IS STRIPPED OF HIS GARMENTS

The procession reaches Calvary, and the prisoners lay down their crosses. Simon is pushed aside by the soldiers for his task is finished. He has to stand back as Jesus is stripped of his clothing, but having shared that long painful journey he cannot leave Him now.

Jesus must have felt so alone as He stood there, exposed in nakedness to all the passers-by. He must have called upon all His inner strength and prayed to His Father to help Him endure this ordeal.

Jesus understands the cross of embarrassment. Through the centuries others have also experienced this indignity. We hope they were able to endure it by remembering the fate of their Saviour. It is sure to happen again, and here and now, we pray that those people too will be sustained by recalling how Jesus bore this insult.

11. JESUS IS NAILED TO THE CROSS

Simon can't take his eyes off Jesus, and he watches in dismay the terrible preparations for crucifixion. Mary, Jesus' mother, is standing nearby and Simon sees her being supported by a young man, who must be one of Jesus' friends.

Alongside Jesus, two thieves were also crucified. One of them refused to accept his punishment, and died cursing Jesus. The other thief confessed his guilt and turned to Jesus in faith. He was rewarded that very day with Jesus' promise of paradise.

All of us want to get to heaven and receive a crown. Are we just as eager to carry our cross? There can be no crown without a cross. The cross must always precede the crown.

12. JESUS DIES ON THE CROSS

Simon stays close to the cross and he hears the scornful remarks addressed to Jesus by some of the passers-by. "He claimed to be the Messiah," they sneer. Simon gazes up at the man on the cross, the man with whom he shared that arduous journey. Can He really be the Messiah?

Jesus hangs on the cross for three hours, but Simon does not leave Him. "If only I had known Him earlier," he says to himself. "How much I could have learned from Him." Now all Simon can do is pray that his friend's sufferings will soon be ended. He hears Jesus cry out in torment, "My God, my God, why have you forsaken me?" Then at last He commends His spirit into God's hands and He dies.

As Jesus hung on the cross He felt for one appaling moment the pain of separation from His Father. It was an experience of utter loneliness and abandonment which must have terrified Him. Yet, this was part of the suffering He bore for us.

Jesus understands the cross of isolation and loneliness that many of us have to carry. Let us remember the promise He made us, "I will not leave you orphans; I will come back to you."

13. Jesus is Taken Down from the Cross

Two men, friends of Jesus, arrive at the foot of the cross, bringing ointment and linen cloths for His burial. They start to take Jesus down from the cross and Simon steps forward to help once more. Mary in her own way thanks him for all his kindness to her Son, and she and the other women begin the sad task of anointing Jesus' body.

It was Jesus' faithful friends who followed Him on his last journey and stood with Him at the foot of His cross. His mother was there, and His beloved disciple, John, with Mary Magdalene, Nicodemus and Joseph. They shared a love of Jesus and so they shared the cross of losing Him. Jesus Himself knew the pain of losing a friend. He wept over the death of His own friend Lazarus. He knows the value of shared friendship, for He says, "Where two or three are gathered together in my name, there am I in the midst of them."

14. Jesus is Buried

Jesus is to be buried in the tomb provided by Joseph of Arimathea. Simon now follows the little group of friends as they carry Jesus away to be buried. He feels a part of that group, having shared so much of Jesus' last few hours. The tomb is sealed with a heavy stone, and Simon leaves the sorrowful women there and quietly goes away, reflecting on all that he has experienced.

In spite of what Jesus Himself had told them, many of His friends and disciples did not think that He would rise again on the third day. The Resurrection came as a great surprise to them. As He was laid in the tomb, many of His followers must have borne a heavy cross of despair, believing that this was the end of all their dreams.

When our loved ones die we are tempted to ask the questions, "Where have they gone? Are they happy?" Our faith is tested, and yet, it is at these moments that our faith is our only effective consolation. Jesus asks us to hold on to our faith in a future life, and He reassures us with these comforting words, "There are many rooms in my Father's house. I am going now to prepare a place for you, and I shall return to take you with me, so that where I am you may be too."

Conclusion

When Simon of Cyrene arrived in Jerusalem that day, he had no idea he would become a follower of Jesus. We have no record of Simon's life after Good Friday, but the events he witnessed must have profoundly affected him. Simon was offered a distasteful cross which at first he resisted but then willingly accepted. We know that his sons, Alexander and Rufus, later became disciples. Jesus might well have said of Simon, "You did not choose me, no, I chose you; and I commissioned you to go out to bear fruit." Let us look forward to the day of our resurrection when we shall be able to thank Jesus for dying on the cross for us and also to thank Simon for the part he played in our salvation.

Joining the
People of the Gospel
on the Way of the Cross

Today we are making the way of the cross in the company of some of those people who witnessed at first hand the trial and death of Jesus. They are the people of the Gospel. Some of them were powerful people, some very ordinary. They responded to Jesus in different ways. Jesus loved each one of them. He died for them, and for each one of us. May we always respond to Him with love and gratitude.

1.   JESUS IS CONDEMNED TO DEATH

I am Pontius Pilate, Governor of the Roman province of Judaea. It's my responsibility to control this turbulent country on Caesar's behalf. A man named Jesus has been brought before me for trial. The Jewish High Priest, Caiaphas, sent him, saying that He is some kind of trouble-maker from Nazareth who stirs up rebellion and claims to be a king. I questioned the man myself, and I found Him very knowledgeable. He told me that I only had authority over Him because it came from above. When I asked Him if He was a king, He gave a strange answer, saying that His kingdom is not of this world. There was something about Him that convinced me He was no criminal. He made attempt to defend Himself. It seems He was destined to die at my hands and those of His people. My wife told me today that she had had a dream about Him and that I should have nothing to do with that innocent man. I find all of this very extraordinary. I handed him back to His own people, telling them firmly that I could find no case against Him, but they were not satisfied and angrily demanded that He be put to death. I tried to release Jesus by offering them Barabbas, that murderous scoundrel, or Jesus. I couldn't believe it when they asked for the release of Barabbas. I thought that after a flogging they would have mercy on Him. In fact it made them more angry. They were like animals at the sight of blood wanting even more. I know that in justice I should set Him free, but now the situation is becoming dangerous. They are saying that I would be no friend of Caesar if I release Jesus. Why should I risk my position for this man? So, although my conscience troubles me, I'll hand Jesus over to be crucified.

2. JESUS RECEIVES HIS CROSS

I am Barabbas, the man reprieved for the Passover, in accordance with our Jewish custom. I was condemned to death for robbery and murder. Today I was expecting to be taken out of my prison cell only to be crucified, but now I find myself out in the street, a free man. I keep telling myself. "I can't believe my luck. I can't believe it." I can't understand why I was chosen instead of this man Jesus. I could see that the crowd had no love for me, but why did they hate Jesus and want Him dead? He seems to be some kind of religious leader, certainly no criminal, yet here He is, standing patiently as the cross is placed on His shoulders. That should have been me. I should be carrying that cross. I can't take my eyes off Jesus. He seems almost willing to take up the cross, that heavy ugly instrument of torture which ought to be on my shoulders at this moment, for I deserve it. Yet I am free, because Jesus has taken my place and is suffering my punishment. I'll never know why, but I know I shall never forget Him. I'll always be grateful to Him.

3. JESUS FALLS THE FIRST TIME

My name is Marcus and I'm a Roman soldier. I haven't been with this unit very long, and I'm the youngest. Today, for the first time, I'm part of an execution squad. We've three prisoners to escort, two of them thieves and the third a man names Jesus. I know His name because I was there when He was flogged on Pontius Pilate's instructions, but I don't know what crime He has committed. They say He claimed to be some sort of king, so after He'd been flogged some of the soldiers began mocking Him, putting a purple robe round His shoulders and a crown of thorns on His head. They blindfolded Him, jeered and spat at Him, and hitting Him with a rod, asked Him who it was who struck Him. Throughout their horse play He seemed so noble and dignified that I felt sorry for Him, and I hung back. But one of the other men said, "Come on, lad, it's only a bit of fun," and it seemed easier just to join in the laughter. Now I see Jesus stumble and fall, and again

I pity Him. That severe flogging must have weakened Him. I saw the metal barbs tearing his flesh. And the cross is so heavy it took two of us to lift it onto His shoulder. Yet, He gets to His feet again without complaining, and seems willing to move on.

4. JESUS MEETS HIS MOTHER

I am Mary, the mother of Jesus. I can hardly recognise my Son, so brutally beaten and tortured. On His head is a crown of thorns. His eyes are half closed with pain blocking out as much light as possible. He moves unsteadily forward as He struggles to carry His cross. I can see the blood staining His robe, the one I made for Him. His back is bleeding from the many lashes the soldiers gave Him. His hands and shoulder are already sore from the friction of the rough wooden cross. That cross looks so heavy, I wonder how He can bear it. I know it is only His strong will and determination which enable Him to persevere. My Son and I have always been so close, and now I can feel His pain. As the procession comes nearer, I manage to push my way through the crowd and get to Jesus. He pauses and raises His head to look at me, opening His eyes fully. Even the soldiers pause to allow us a moment together. His look tells me everything – His pain, His sadness and His love. We clasp hands and I know I'm giving Him some comfort and encouragement. In return, He strengthens me. He tried so many times to prepare me for this day, and although it breaks my heart to see Him suffering like this, I know it's His way of doing His Father's will. Now, the soldiers move their prisoners on, taking my Son away from me.

5. THE CROSS IS LAID UPON SIMON OF CYRENE

My name is Simon. I'm originally from Cyrene, but now I live outside Jerusalem and I've come into the city today on business. When I arrived there was a huge crowd of people on the street. There seemed to be some kind of procession taking place, so out of curiosity I came to have a look. I soon realised what was happening. Three men are on their way to be crucified, each carrying his own cross. One of the men is in a dreadful condition. He's obviously been flogged, and someone has made fun of Him by placing a crown of thorns on His head, which must cause Him even more pain. He looks ready to collapse. Suddenly, I see the Roman centurion on horseback pointing in my direction, and two soldiers seize my arms and drag me forward, saying I must help this prisoner carry His cross to Calvary. I refuse indignantly. I feel sorry for this poor criminal, but why should I get involved? These soldiers are bullies are well-armed. What resistance can I offer? None. So, thinking of my own safety and my family at home, I obey them. The prisoner turns to look at me, not angrily or resentfully, but with enormous gratitude. As I move nearer to Him to take some of the weight of the cross, I can sense that there is great goodness in this man. Even though I know nothing about this man I am convinced that He is innocent. I really want to help Him. I can't explain it, but I feel privileged to be here, sharing some of His suffering.

6.   VERONICA WIPES THE FACE OF JESUS

My name is Veronica, and I live here in Jerusalem. I've heard about this man Jesus who is being crucified today. They say He is a good man who helped people, yet the High Priests want Him put to death. I heard the procession coming, so I've come out to see it, just to catch a glimpse of Jesus. Now I see Him, moving slowly and painfully up the hill behind two other prisoners. In the heat of the day He looks totally exhausted. His face is covered in sweat and dirt, and streaked with blood, for someone has placed on His head a crown made of thorns. I feel so sorry for Him, and I quickly run back into my house to dip a towel in cold water and bring it to Him to wash His face. It's not much, but I know it will refresh Him. Without thinking of the Roman soldiers guarding the prisoners, I run to Jesus and place my towel gently on His face. He smiles at me and thanks me so kindly. He is so grateful for that small act of kindness. I remove my towel, and to my amazement the image of Jesus' face is imprinted on it. I stare at the towel, scarcely able to believe my eyes. I look back at Jesus, but already the soldiers are hurrying Him away. Now I know in my heart that this man is someone very special.

7.   JESUS FALLS THE SECOND TIME

I am Mary, once a prostitute, and Jesus is my friend. He saved me from an immoral life and I can never repay Him for all His kindness. When I heard that he had been arrested and condemned to death I just had to come and be near Him. I have joined the crowd, keeping close to Mary, His mother and John, and I'm following the procession to Calvary. I know that Jesus is laying down His life for us all, but it's terrible to see Him suffering. He is finding it so difficult to carry the burden of the cross, and now He staggers and falls a second time. I remember the first time I met Jesus. It was at the home of Simon the Pharisee. I was so conscious of the sinful life I was leading, but I had heard of Jesus and wanted so much to meet Him. I fell at His feet, wetting them with my tears and wiping them with my hair. I brought some expensive oils with which to anoint His head. One of His disciples complained, saying that it was a waste of money, but Jesus praised me for what I had done. He said I was anointing His body for burial, but I never thought then that one day I would witness His death. I know He is suffering for my sins. It is my sins that make Him fall. How I wish at this moment I could touch Him again and Him I love Him. Now I can see Him struggling to His feet again, determined to finish this journey.

8.   Jesus meets the women of Jerusalem

My name is Esther. I live here in Jerusalem and I have often heard Jesus preaching, and seen Him walking amongst the people. He listens to all of our problems, comforts us, and heals those who are sick. We women know how much He loves us and we love Him in return, because He is so good. He genuinely loved our children and made time for them. One day, when He was preaching, He took my little boy onto His lap and put His arms around Him, and said, "Let the little children come to me, for of such is the kingdom of heaven." I didn't know what He meant, but I understood that He cared about us. So, I've come here today with some of my friends, because we've heard that Jesus is going to be crucified and we don't know why. The procession comes closer, and I step out in front of it, beckoning my friends to follow me. I don't care about the Roman soldiers, I just want to see Jesus for one last time. He sees us standing here weeping, and He stops to speak to us. As always, He thinks about us first. "Don't weep for me," He says, "but for yourselves.". He tries to warn us about terrible things which are going to happen in the future, but all I can think about is today, when our dear friend is being taken from us, though He has done nothing wrong. The soldiers push us all back into the crowd, and I can only watch Jesus slowly walking away.

9. JESUS FALLS THE THIRD TIME

I am Reuben, and I am a thief. I've been a petty criminal all my life, and I've no regrets. The only thing I regret is that this time I got caught and sentenced to death. I'm on my way to be crucified, along with another thief called Dismas and a man named Jesus. I know nothing about Jesus, except that some people say he is the Messiah. If that's true why is He here with us? We are all suffering agony from the weight of the cross we have to carry. The heat of the blazing sun makes us all feel faint and dizzy. Yet Jesus seems to be attracting all the sympathy. Already He's had help with carrying His cross, and then a woman from the crowd came to Him and washed His face. No-one did that for me. No-one seems to care about me. I just have to struggle on alone. Jesus has fallen twice during this journey, and now I see Him down on his knees again. If He really is the Messiah, why doesn't He save Himself, and save us at the same time? But He forces Himself to stand up and carry on, as if He actually wants to die. The man's an enigma to me.

10. JESUS IS STRIPPED OF HIS GARMENTS

I am Mary, still following my Son Jesus on His last dreadful journey. Jesus has now reached the hill of Calvary where He is to be nailed to His cross. Not content with torturing Him, His executioners are now humiliating Him by stripping Him of His clothes. They work quickly and cruelly. Jesus flinches as they pull the clothing from His back. I think back to His childhood and remember the many times I had lovingly undressed Him for bed or for a bath. Then, I never thought it would come to all this. How embarrassing it must be for my Jesus standing there naked before the gawping crowd. How I would love to cover Him in my arms.

11. JESUS IS NAILED TO THE CROSS

I am Mary of Magdala. I'm trying to be brave. I'm doing my best to hold back my tears. But now I can't bear to see what the soldiers are going to do to Jesus. One of them has a nail about five inches long in one hand and a heavy hammer in the other. Two other soldiers drag Jesus down onto His cross. I just feel like interfering, getting Jesus to His feet and grabbing the nail and hammer so that it can't be used. I've got to get control of myself or I can see the soldiers grabbing hold of me and telling me to clear off. Jesus looks up to heaven. He must be praying for the strength to endure this brutal torture. One soldier opens the hand of Jesus and stamps his foot on it. The soldier holding the nail and hammer crouches down and poises the nail over Jesus' wrist and begins hammering. I can't bear this sight and I turn away. I block my ears, but I can still hear the hammering. After some silence it continues again as they repeat this torture to the other hand and then to His feet. I now can look at Jesus as they raise the cross to secure it in the ground. I can see the pain on His face, not a sound has come from Him. How I would like to wash His feet once again with my tears and wipe them with my hair. If I can't do that now I shall when He is taken down from the cross to be buried.

12. JESUS DIES ON THE CROSS

I am Benjamin, a bystander. Suddenly there is an eerie atmosphere. The shouting and jeering has stopped and all is quiet. A strange silence has descended on the earth. Every minute it seems to be getting darker and darker and the clouds heavier and heavier as though a storm is ready to break. I've followed this procession from the start because I've heard so much about Jesus, and the whole execution has intrigued me. I wonder who He really is. Above the silence Jesus is heard to whisper, "I thirst". I can imagine how parched He must be due to the heat and loss of blood. His tongue must be swollen and dry as desert sand. A cup of cool water would be such a solace at this moment. I'll do what I can for Him. There is a jar of sour wine here provided for the dying men. I rush and find a branch, attach a sponge to it and dip it into the wine. I then put it to Jesus' lips to bring Him some relief. He allows the sponge to touch His lips. Now with all the strength He can muster He cries aloud, "Eli, Eli, lama sabachthani?", meaning, "My God, my God, why have you forsaken me?" Some of the onlookers think He is calling on Elijah to save Him. He must be in the depths of despair. But very quickly His mood changes to one of triumph as He whispers, "It is finished". He looks up to heaven as though He is waiting for someone to receive Him. It must be His heavenly Father for it is into His hands that He commends His spirit as He bows His head and dies.

13. JESUS IS TAKEN DOWN FROM THE CROSS

My name is Nicodemus. I can claim to be a secret disciple of Jesus. I never had the courage to come to Him by day. I visited Him secretly by night. Being a Pharisee I was afraid of what my peers would think. Now looking back I wish I had been brave enough to have supported Him openly. Now I'll do for Him what little I can. I've brought the most expensive ointments I could buy for anointing Him, and also the shroud in which to wrap His body. I shall give these to His mother and the women so that they can prepare Him for burial. Mary accepts my gift quietly, but I can see from her look how immensely grateful she is. The three men present, John, Joseph and myself take Jesus from Mary's lap. We, place Him on the ground and Mary and the women begin anointing His body. They have to work quickly because the Sabbath is due to begin. They then wrap His body in the shroud, and we men carry Him to the place of burial.

14. JESUS IS BURIED

I am Joseph of Arimathea, a man of great wealth. I remember Jesus talking about riches. He said, "How hard it is for a rich man to enter the kingdom of God". He emphasised this point by adding, "It is easier for a camel to pass through the eye of a needle than for a rich man to enter the kingdom of heaven". Those words impressed me greatly. It taught me to put my wealth to good purposes and to be detached from my possessions. I've prepared for myself a tomb in a garden not far from here. I'll show the lesson of detachment I've learnt and I'll give my burial place to Jesus. Up to now He has been treated with hatred and contempt. At least now I can give Him a dignified burial, one He so richly deserves. I tell Mary of my plans and she thanks me. With great devotion we take His body and lay it in the tomb. Mary and the women lovingly embrace Him for the last time and we roll the stone against the entrance of the tomb and go our separate ways.

The Way of the Cross with Judas

INTRODUCTION

Jesus said, "The Son of Man is going His appointed way, but alas for the man by whom He is betrayed. It were better if this man had never been born". That man was Judas Iscariot. And today we are making the Way of the Cross in his company.

1. JESUS IS CONDEMNED TO DEATH

I am Judas, once a follower of Jesus. It's my fault that Jesus is here on trial in front of the Roman governor, Pontius Pilate. The chief priests and the Pharisees always hated Jesus. He was forever challenging what they stood for. He was winning the hearts of so many people and now they were looking for a way to get rid of Him. It was I who gave him up to them. Why did I do it? I love this man Jesus, but He wasn't the kind of Messiah I had in mind. I wanted Him to be a real leader, helping us to overthrow the Romans who rule our land. But He talked all the time of another kingdom, not of this world. Some of the other disciples argued about who would hold high positions in that kingdom, but there didn't seem to be a place for me there. I've always been the outsider, the only Judean amongst all those Galileans. Because I was disillusioned I went to the High Priest and offered him Jesus of Nazareth. I never thought it would come to this. Even Pilate could see that He was guilty of no crime. He wanted to release Jesus, but the High Priest told him he would be no friend of Caesar. Knowing that his position as Governor was in jeopardy, Pilate washed his hands of the whole affair and handed Jesus over to them to be crucified.

2. JESUS RECEIVES HIS CROSS

Pilate could have saved Him. The people of Jerusalem, who had witnessed so many of His kind deeds, could have saved Him. It wasn't all my fault. But perhaps I am more guilty because I started the train of events which have brought Jesus here. A party of Roman soldiers is now taking charge of Jesus, along with two other condemned men, both thieves. They place the heavy cross on Jesus' shoulder, and He accepts it without a struggle. Even now, He could save Himself if He wanted to, but it seems as if He really wants to die. In spite of what I've done, I can't quite leave Jesus, so I'm going to follow the procession, along with this huge crowd of curious spectators.

3. JESUS FALLS THE FIRST TIME

Jesus is finding it difficult to carry His cross and He falls for the first time. Earlier this morning He was flogged, and He has lost a lot of blood. My conscience begins to trouble me, because I can see what I have done to my friend Jesus. I remember the first time I let Him down. He made me treasurer of the common purse, the money we used to help the poor. I stole money from those funds. Jesus knew what I was doing, but He never said a word to the others. He wanted me to have every opportunity to pay back the money, but I betrayed His trust. I wonder whether He remembers that now, as He struggles to His feet. I could so easily have been one of those two thieves, paying the penalty for the crime of theft, while Jesus, who is innocent, is taking the punishment I deserve.

4. JESUS MEETS HIS MOTHER

I knew Mary would stay close to Jesus. She was so loyal and His first disciple. She doesn't notice me, but I can see her now, quietly moving towards Jesus to try to comfort Him. I know how her heart is hurting, for no one loves Him as she does. I know Mary well, because she always welcomed me into her home as one of Jesus' friends In fact, she treated me as a son, but I know the love she and Jesus have for each other is something very special. Jesus once said that anyone who does the will of His Father in heaven is His kin. I would have liked to belong to that family, but now I've cut myself off once and for all.

5. THE CROSS IS LAID UPON SIMON OF CYRENE

It is obvious that Jesus cannot carry this cross alone. The soldiers want to hurry Him on, so they take hold of a man standing in the crowd and they are making him take up Jesus' cross to help Him. My heart goes out to Jesus. I want to help Him, too, but I can't reach Him now. I couldn't look Him in the face after what I have done, and I know He would not want me anywhere near Him. Instead, I have to watch this stranger receiving Jesus' thanks and love.

6. VERONICA WIPES THE FACE OF JESUS

Jesus looks exhausted, and He pauses to get His breath. A woman approaches Him, paying no attention to the armed escort. She carries a clean white cloth and she starts to wipe Jesus' face, cleaning away the sweat and blood. He looks at her kindly and gratefully. I envy her that look. She's never met Jesus before, but she can get close to Him and help to ease His suffering, while I am on the outside. I have made myself a stranger to Him and He cannot love me now. The woman is rewarded not only by Jesus' thanks, but also with a miracle. As she starts to fold up her cloth she finds the image of Jesus' face on it.

7. JESUS FALLS THE SECOND TIME

With the heat of the sun and the heavy weight of the cross, Jesus is soon bathed in sweat again, and falls to His knees. But after a few moments He finds the strength to get up and carry on with His journey. If only I had such determination. I struggled against temptation for a while, but not hard enough. I have to admit to myself that I was always on the fringe. I would have liked to have been one of the special three. My envy and resentment drove me to go to the High Priest to ask him what he would give me in exchange for Jesus. He gave me thirty pieces of silver. Is it the thought of my disloyalty that weighs heavily on Jesus at this moment causing Him to fall?

8. JESUS MEETS THE WOMEN OF JERUSALEM

Several local women are standing watching the procession, weeping in sympathy for Jesus. I want to weep too, seeing what I have done to my friend. Women seem to be attracted to Jesus, perhaps because of His kindness and gentleness. I know how much Martha and Mary love Him, and Mary Magdalene, too. They weren't afraid to show Him their love, but I hesitated so often, and missed so many opportunities. Jesus tells the women they should weep for themselves, not for Him, because terrible destruction is coming to Jerusalem. He can see the future. He can see into people's hearts. Perhaps He foresaw my betrayal.

9. Jesus Falls the Third Time

Jesus is almost within sight of Calvary, and He falls again, the worst fall yet. The soldiers look at Him, obviously wondering whether He will be able to walk the last few yards. His face shows pain, but also a look of resignation, just as He did in the Garden of Gethsemane when He saw me approaching with the High Priest's servants. At that moment He said to me, "Friend, would you betray the Son of Man with a kiss?" Even at this late hour I could have said, I'm sorry, Lord," but I didn't. My kiss identified Him, and brought Him to this dreadful death. Yet, He doesn't flinch from death, but gets to His feet again and slowly walks towards the place where He is to be crucified.

10. Jesus is Stripped of His Garments

On the hill of Calvary, the crosses are placed on the ground, and Jesus and the two thieves are stripped of their clothes. I can see that Jesus' back and shoulders are lacerated by the scourging He was given earlier today, and now He is exposed to the crowd in the utmost degradation and mockery. This is what I have done to Him. Jesus is being exhibited to the world, while my shame and guilt remain hidden, like the thirty silver coins in my pocket.

11. Jesus is Nailed to the Cross

The crowd falls silent as the three condemned men are fastened to their crosses. There is only the sound of hammer on nail, and cries of terror and pain from the two thieves. Jesus doesn't resist or cry out. He just offers Himself to His executioners and allows them to drive nails into His hands and feet. Is this what He meant when He said at supper last night, "This is my body which will be given up for you?" He knew even then that I would betray Him. I will never forget that moment when He handed me the bread across the table and said, "Do quickly what you have to do." Now, as the cross is raised, I can see exactly what I have done, and I have the pain of knowing that I can never undo it.

12. JESUS DIES ON THE CROSS

At the foot of the cross I can see those people who were always close to Jesus – His mother, Mary, of course, and the other two Mary's, and John, the disciple He loved. It was John who discovered from Jesus Himself that I would be the traitor, so he will certainly have no love for me.

People are starting to mock Jesus as they pass by His cross. They cannot believe that this wounded, helpless man is really the Messiah. Obviously He could not be the Messiah. What good could He do nailed to a cross? Jesus prays for them, that they will be forgiven for their cruelty and ignorance. Many times I have seen Him pray for people who needed forgiveness. I wish with all my heart that I could ask for His forgiveness now, but I know that what I have done can never be pardoned. I cannot even forgive myself.

The two thieves are talking to Jesus. One of them sneers at Him, challenging Him to save Himself and them by coming down from the cross. The other man seems to have faith in Jesus, saying to Him, "Remember me when you come into your kingdom." And Jesus replies, "My friend, I promise you this very day you will be with me in paradise." This thief, who has only known Jesus for a few hours, is to share paradise with Him. All his crimes are forgiven. But I am not just a thief, I am guilty of the death of my greatest friend, so for me there can be no forgiveness, no place in the kingdom. I feel those thirty silver coins in my pocket, and I am filled with despair.

Jesus looks tenderly at His mother and gives her into the care of John, His closest disciple. I could have been a member of that loving family, but I've cut myself off from love. I shall be an outsider forever.

Jesus, in His last agony, cries out, "It is finished", and He dies. It is finished for me, too. The only good thing I can do is to give back the thirty pieces of silver. Perhaps in that way I could redeem myself.

13. Jesus is taken down from the cross

The Sabbath is approaching, and the body of Jesus is quickly taken down from the cross. I recognise two wealthy friends of Jesus, Joseph of Arimathea and Nicodemus, bringing fine cloths and ointment, so that He may be given a dignified burial. These friends have remained loyal to Jesus to the very end, while I, who owed Him so much, gave Him into the hands of His enemies. How sad His mother looks, yet somehow peaceful, too, as if she truly believes His sacrifice was worthwhile.

14. Jesus is buried

I follow the quiet procession as Jesus is carried away to be buried. His resting place is to be the tomb of Joseph of Arimathea, in a garden not far from Calvary. A stone is rolled across the entrance to the tomb, and then His mother and friends silently go away. Jesus of Nazareth is crucified, dead and buried, because I did not love Him as He loved me. If He is really the Messiah, then in three days' time He will roll back this stone and rise again. But for me there is no hope. I will return the money the chief priest gave me, and then I will put an end to my life.

Conclusion

Jesus, we thank you for allowing us to make the Way of the Cross, accompanied by Judas. Like him, there are still people who despair and believe that their sins are too great to be forgiven. We pray for them, and that like the Good Thief, even at the eleventh hour, there is always forgiveness for them if only they would turn to you and say, "Lord, remember me in your kingdom."

We've all wondered Lord if Judas, with the noose round his neck, before he threw himself to the ground said, "I'm sorry, Jesus." We hope he did, and should he need our prayers at this moment, we ask you to give him a place in your kingdom.

Satan pursues Jesus to Calvary

INTRODUCTION

My name is Satan, the Evil One. I was once Lucifer, an archangel. They tell me that it was through pride that I rebelled against God and with other angels who supported me I was cast into hell for all eternity. You may be surprised that I am making this journey to Calvary with Jesus. So many people nowadays don't believe in Hell or in me. That makes everything so much easier for me. I can move around freely without being noticed. You may not recognise me, but I exist!

Ever since I was thrown out of Heaven I have had only one desire: to take my revenge on God by destroying what He loves most, the men and women He created. This man Jesus is especially favoured by God, but now I've got Him in my power and I'm going to enjoy seeing Him suffer.

1. JESUS IS CONDEMNED TO DEATH

The High Priests are happy now that Pilate has condemned Jesus to death. Pilate washes his hands of the whole affair as he brings Jesus out to be crucified. I feel very satisfied with my work, for of course the whole thing is a plot devised by me. I filled the High Priests' hearts with envy and malice. I gave Pilate a good dose of cowardice. I even used that poor fool Judas to betray Jesus. It was so easy to manipulate them all! And now Jesus stands here silently, waiting for his executioners.

2.   JESUS RECEIVES HIS CROSS

The Roman soldiers place a heavy cross on Jesus' shoulders and prepare for this journey to Calvary. I don't like Jesus' attitude. Look at Him, accepting His cross so willingly. I wish He'd curse it like the two thieves who are also being crucified today. I know I shall have the pleasure of dragging these two men down to my domain, but you watch before this journey's over I'll break this Jesus. I am the one who has organised all this, just as I did in the Garden of Eden. Why should Adam and Eve enjoy the happiness from which I was excluded? I couldn't allow that, so I tempted them to believe they could be as powerful as God by disobeying Him. They fell for my lies so willingly and now the whole human race carries the burden of sin and death. Is there any one who can redeem them? Does Jesus think that by carrying this cross He is going to save them? If this is how He thinks let me tell you that I am going to destroy Him.

3.   JESUS FALLS THE FIRST TIME

I've taken a close interest in Jesus ever since He was born. God threatened to send a saviour into the world who would crush my head and I've wondered whether this Jesus might be the one, but seeing Him now, beaten and humiliated I know it can't be Him. Still, I've watched Him carefully attacking Him whenever I could. I see Him falling now under the weight of His cross, and I remember the first time I tried to destroy Him. It was when He was a baby. There was something unusual about His birth in Bethlehem, so I gave Herod the idea of having every male baby murdered. Somehow I was tricked and Jesus and His family escaped into Egypt. I now see Jesus getting to His feet again and continuing the journey. I've got to give it to Him, He's got stamina.

4.   JESUS MEETS HIS SORROWFUL MOTHER

We haven't gone far before I notice Mary, the mother of Jesus. This woman makes me very uneasy. She is so good and innocent as Eve was before I deceived her, but I have never been able to pervert Mary's goodness. I remember God's promise that a woman would be the cause of my downfall by bearing a saviour. If ever a mother and son have frustrated my plans it has been these two. Because of this I hate them. I have never been able to get near them. Now Mary moves close to Jesus, no doubt trying to comfort Him, but I shall soon see her weeping. They have a few moments together before the soldiers move Jesus along.

5.   The cross is laid upon Simon of Cyrene

Jesus is so weakened that it seems if He is going to reach Calvary He will need some help. The soldiers have dragged a man out of the crowd and are making him bear some of the weight of the cross. At first this man is reluctant, of course, but now he seems to be taking up the burden quite willingly. How contemptible, to serve in this way! Has he so little pride? I will never serve anyone.

6.   Veronica wipes the face of Jesus

The procession continues and it is very pleasing to see Jesus sweating and struggling under His cross. But now there is a delay as a woman from the crowd approaches Him and starts wiping His face with a towel, cleaning away the blood and sweat and dirt. Such a pointless gesture! I wonder why she chose Him and ignored the two thieves? Now the woman takes back the towel and there seems to be a strange mark on it, almost like an imprint of His own face. Here He is again, exercising this power which He seems to get from somewhere. There are still things about this man that I just don't understand.

7.   Jesus falls the second time

Jesus is on His knees for the second time, and this reminds me of my second attack on Him. It was after Jesus had been baptised in the Jordan that I encountered Him in the desert. I wanted to find out for myself just who He was. Was He the Son of God? Was He the saviour who was to crush my head? I asked Him this three times. I tried all the usual human weaknesses – greed, ambition, pride – but He resisted all my temptations. He told me in no uncertain terms to go. If He is the Son of God, He could have proved it by calling on God's power, but He refused. He would not tell me what I needed to know, so in the end I had to leave Him alone only for a while. And now here He is, recovering His strength and stubbornly walking on again.

8. JESUS MEETS THE WOMEN OF JERUSALEM

Another obstacle halts the procession. It's a group of wailing women, lamenting over Jesus. Well, they can't save Him now. Let them give up all hope, as we in Hell have done. I will give them some of my despair. One thought consoles me: if by any chance Jesus is God's Son, then God and all His angels must be weeping too as they see Him suffering and so close to death. He speaks to the women, making some kind of prophecy about the destruction of Jerusalem, but now the soldiers push them aside so that the prisoners can move on.

9. JESUS FALLS THE THIRD TIME

Again Jesus falls, as He is now quite exhausted. This fall reminds me that I had a third opportunity to test Him. It wasn't very long ago when He was praying in the Garden of Gethsemane. All His friends had fallen asleep. He had a moment of weakness and I seized my chance. I made Him so afraid that His sweat was like drops of blood and He prayed to God to rescue Him from death. What agony He suffered! I thought I could have destroyed Him then, but He chose to do God's will and I lost my hold over Him. By the time Judas arrived with the High Priest's servants, He had found His strength, and I had to leave Him again. And now I see Him once more finding that same determination to get up and go on. Is it possible that God is sustaining Him through His final journey?

10. JESUS IS STRIPPED OF HIS GARMENTS

He doesn't look much like the Son of God now, stripped of His clothes, helpless and vulnerable. His body is sore and bleeding and He stands there patiently, like a lamb waiting to be slaughtered. I love it, I love it! Most of His friends have abandoned Him. He has lost everything now. I, too, lost everything when I lost Heaven. All I wanted was to reign in equal power with God, and because of my rebellion I was banished to Hell. My only happiness now is in getting even. If Jesus is the Son of God my revenge is complete, for I have brought Him to this place, and He is soon going to die.

11. Jesus is nailed to the cross

The soldiers place the three crosses on the ground and start to fasten each prisoner to his cross. Jesus meekly stretches out His arms allowing the soldiers to nail His wrists to the wood. I am amazed at His bravery. Not a cry of protest or a shriek of pain comes from His lips. Perhaps He realises He is finished now, there is nothing more He can do. There are cries of pain and fear from the two thieves. The pain of crucifixion will be nothing compared with the pain of Hell which awaits all three of these men.

12. Jesus dies on the cross

The crosses are now raised up. Very few of Jesus' friends have stayed with Him, but His wretched mother is still here, weeping and whinging at the foot of the cross. Many passers-by jeer at Him, saying, "If you are the Messiah, save yourself." I'm glad to see there is so little faith in Him. One of the thieves challenges Him to save them all. The other thief silences him, and turns to Jesus saying, "Remember me when you come into your kingdom." Jesus responds by promising him a place in paradise. He doesn't have the power to make such a promise. The man's a sinner, destined for Hell, but now…I can feel him slipping from my grasp.

I won't feel really safe until Jesus is dead. Surely He can't last much longer? This is my moment of triumph. I'm beginning to rub my hands in glee. I can't wait to begin my victory dance. Jesus, the so-called Son of God will soon be dead, and everyone who believed in Him will be in despair. Then the world will know that I have conquered. I lost the battle in Heaven, but I shall be the winner here. I sense His weakness, and I make one more attack on Him. He cries out, "My God, my God, why have you forsaken me?" We struggle together, and I am winning.

Now I feel something terrifying is happening. Jesus exclaims, "It is finished!" He bows His head and dies, and suddenly the whole world is shaken. A violent storm breaks overhead. There is an earthquake, and the dead rise from their graves. Now I realise that Jesus is the Son of God. He has won and I have lost. It was all true-all those prophecies, all the things He said about Himself. He has crushed my head. He is the Saviour of the world, and I no longer hold the world in my power. Now for all eternity I shall be kicking myself saying, "Why didn't I realise that this was the way God had planned to save mankind?"

13. JESUS IS TAKEN DOWN FROM THE CROSS

The Roman soldiers return to remove the bodies from their crosses. They break the legs of the two thieves, but Jesus is already dead. Two men now arrive, apparently disciples of Jesus, and take down His body to prepare it for burial. I remember another prophecy concerning Jesus, that He would rise from the dead and so conquer death. I can only wait anxiously to see whether this promise will also be fulfiled.

14. JESUS IS BURIED

I watch the little group of companions carrying Jesus away to be buried. He is placed in a tomb in the rock, secured by a heavy stone across the entrance, and His friends go away sorrowfully. Their sorrow cannot be compared to the anguish I feel as my power is weakened. I know where Jesus is now. He has gone to open the gates of heaven for all those souls who escaped my clutches. Will He rise on the third day? I shall wait and see. But all is not lost. Jesus may be beyond my reach. He may have won this battle, but men and women still have their free will and I can influence them. I still have strength to get them in my grasp. Wherever I can spread hatred, envy and despair in people's souls, wherever I can replace faith with doubt, those souls will be with me, in Hell for all eternity.

CONCLUSION

Heavenly Father, we thank you for planning our redemption. We thank Jesus, for the depth of His love and bravery. We know Satan is very powerful and still very eager to take us to his kingdom, but with you on our side we can resist his power. May we all one day hear from our Saviour's lips the words, "I promise you this day you will be with me in paradise."

The Way of the Cross for Children

1. JESUS IS CONDEMNED TO DEATH

Picture Pilate sitting in the court room wearing his judge's robes. Jesus stands quietly in front of him waiting for his decision. Pilate knows that the religious leaders hate Jesus because they won't admit that He is God's Son. Pilate also knows that Jesus has done nothing wrong, but what can he do? If he sets Jesus free there will be a riot and he could lose his job. There is only one thing to do and that is to wash his hands of the whole affair.

There are times when we are accused of something we haven't done. It isn't fair. All we can do is tell the truth and hope that people will believe us. If they don't, we must put up with the unfairness. Jesus was treated in the same way and so He understands how we feel and He will help us.

We pray for all those people who have been judged unfairly.

2. THE CROSS IS LAID UPON JESUS' SHOULDER.

Jesus stands in the street with two thieves who have also been condemned to death. Each man is given his cross to carry. It is a very heavy cross, weighing about 16 stone — heavier than a man like your Dad — and it's made of rough wood. Jesus accepts His cross willingly because He knows that it is through carrying His cross and dying on it that He will save the whole world.

Jesus told us that we could not be His disciples unless we took up our cross every day and followed Him. What kind of cross do we have to carry today? Perhaps someone has been unkind to us. or perhaps we have to cope with lessons we don't like. We can't escape it, so let's remember the picture of Jesus carrying His cross willingly and cheerfully. Our cross will never be as heavy as His and He will help us to carry ours.

We pray for everyone who is finding their cross hard to carry today.

3. JESUS FALLS FOR THE FIRST TIME UNDER THE WEIGHT OF HIS CROSS

Jesus is very weak. He had hardly any sleep last night. The soldiers have whipped Him and crowned Him with thorns and His back and head are sore and bleeding. The road is hard and stony and now the midday sun is unbearably hot. It is not surprising that He stumbles and falls. Imagine Him, God's Son, lying in the dust, His heavy cross on top of Him. Two soldiers lift the cross off Him and another one drags Him to His feet. Jesus steadies Himself, places the cross on His shoulder and tries to carry on.

Sometimes we do things which are wrong. It's the wrong things we do which cause us to fall, but we can't just give up. As soon as we realise that we've done wrong, we must say we are sorry and begin again.

We pray for those who have fallen under their cross and can't find the strength to continue their journey.

4. JESUS MEETS HIS MOTHER

Jesus' Mother Mary is following Him on this painful journey to Calvary, She wouldn't want to be anywhere else. Her heart is broken with sadness. To watch her Son suffer like this is her cross. Jesus must have told her that He was going to die, but she still finds it so hard to see Him treated cruelly. Among the hustle and bustle she manages to get near Him and give Him a hug. This comforts Jesus and gives Him strength and it makes Mary happy to know that before He died she could hold him for the last time.

Mary is our mother too. She loves us in the same way as she loved her Son Jesus. She never wants any harm to come to us. If we are hurt or worried, how often the person we run to is our own mother. Let's get into the habit of running to Mary. our Blessed Mother, when we are unhappy or find ourselves in any kind of trouble. Imagine her putting her arms around you, telling you not to be frightened, wiping your tears and bringing a smile to your face.

We pray for all mothers, especially those who are worried about their children.

5. SIMON OF CYRENE HELPS JESUS TO CARRY HIS CROSS

The soldiers begin to notice Jesus getting weaker and weaker. They wonder if He will be able to complete the journey to Calvary outside the city walls where He is to be crucified. To them He is just another criminal. Why should they help Him? In the crowds lining the street is a man called Simon. He is a strong looking man and one of the soldiers bullies him into carrying Jesus' cross. Simon might not have wanted to get involved, but there was no way he could refuse. Those soldiers might have beaten him or put him in prison, and he had a family back home to think about, his two sons Alexander and Rufus. But Jesus is so glad of his help that He gives him a smile and a word of thanks. This helps Simon to lift Jesus' heavy cross.

When we see someone worse off than ourselves how do we feel? Are we reluctant to help? Can we be bothered? Can we give our time, some necessary help or even some money? Or do we leave others to help them? May the picture of Simon helping Jesus carry His cross remind us to be caring. We can be like Simon to anyone who needs our help.

We pray that we may be always ready to help anyone who has a heavy cross to carry.

6. VERONICA WIPES THE FACE OF JESUS

The heat of the day is making all the prisoners sweat. As Jesus drags His feet along the dusty road a woman living nearby takes pity on Him. She sees sweat and drops of blood trickling down His face. She rushes into her house and wets a clean towel with cool water. Without thinking about the Roman soldiers, she goes straight to Jesus and gently wipes His face. Jesus smiles gratefully. What a surprise she gets when she finds on the towel a picture of Jesus' face! Because of this picture, this woman has been given the name Veronica, which means "true image".

Do we notice when other people are suffering? Are we sometimes so busy with our own lives that we just don't see what is happening around us? The next time we see Mum, Dad a sister or a brother or anyone in pain let us think of ways to help them. We could say a kind word, get them their medicine, or gently rub their head to ease a headache. We might even keep very quiet so that they can rest. It won't cost us anything, but it tells the one who is suffering that we care and we love them. It does help.

We pray for people who are sick and in pain, and for all the kind people who look after them.

7. JESUS FALLS THE SECOND TIME

Jesus is nearly halfway through this painful journey. The heat is weakening him, the wound in His shoulder made by the rough cross has torn His skin. There is a throbbing pain. What a relief it would be just to stop and sit down somewhere and have a cool drink. Instead He stumbles and falls. He even knocks Simon off his balance. Simon goes to help Him and when he has steadied Jesus on His feet the soldiers once again place the cross on their shoulders.

When the cross we carry is to heavy for us, we often fall. Our cross may be doing our homework, keeping our room tidy, putting up with being teased by brothers or sisters. Our teacher may tell us off for not paying attention in class, or Mum may insist that it's time to turn off the TV and go to bed. We grumble and complain. But let's think of all the terrible things Jesus had to endure. Then we'll pick ourselves up, carry our cross cheerfully, and try to do better next time.

We pray for everyone who feels too weak to carry their cross; may Jesus give them His strength.

8. JESUS COMFORTS THE WOMEN OF JERUSALEM

Jesus passes some women with their children. They are crying for Him, because they love Him so much. Jesus does not think of Himself He thinks of them and He can see into the future. He knows what will happen in the year 70, about 37 years from now. The Roman soldiers will invade their city, many will die by the sword, others by starvation from going into hiding. Their homes and their beloved temple will be destroyed. The thought of all their suffering makes Jesus shudder and He says to the women, "Daughters of Jerusalem weep not for me but for yourselves and for your children".

During our lifetime we shall all have to suffer in some way, but there are always people worse off than ourselves. May we, like Jesus, spare them a thought and at least pray for them. This will help us to carry our own cross more willingly and cheerfully.

We pray for people throughout the world who have lost homes and families because of war, disasters or lack of food.

9. JESUS FALLS THE THIRD TIME

Jesus has just got outside the walls of Jerusalem. He has not far to go before He lays down His cross. He can see the hill of Calvary. Climbing this hill is going to be hard because He is so tired. so thirsty and in such great pain. That wound in His shoulder won't go away and His flesh seems to be on fire, He has a thumping headache caused by the thorns that have pricked His head. The light from the sun is so strong that He finds great difficulty in keeping His eyes open. He feels His energy draining away and He falls. He has come so near to the spot where He is about to die and win us a place in heaven. This thought, plus Simon's help, makes Him get up and drag Himself up the hill of Calvary.

One day will be the last day of our life. Let us ask Jesus to help us never give up trying to love God and do good to others. May everything we do be a step in the right direction, taking us towards heaven.

10. JESUS IS STRIPPED OF HIS CLOTHING

At last Jesus has reached the hill of Calvary. What a relief it is for Him to lay down His cross. We can be sure that He thanks Simon again for his help. The soldiers surround Jesus and begin stripping Him of His clothing. How often when He was young His mother Mary undressed Him for bed or for a bath and how loving and gentle she was. Not so the Roman soldiers. They are rough and tear His clothing from Him. Jesus winces for His clothes have stuck to His many wounds from the scourging. Jesus seems so helpless. He just closes His eyes, grinds His teeth and endures the pain. While these soldiers do this to Jesus He just can't stop loving them.

There will be times when other people treat us badly and we feel hopeless and alone. But we know we won't really be alone because Jesus has promised never to leave us. He will be there to help us get through everything difficult or unpleasant.

We pray for people who feel alone because they don't yet know Jesus as their friend.

11. JESUS IS NAILED TO THE CROSS

The cross is laid on the ground and the soldiers make Jesus stand at the foot of it and then two of the soldiers put their arm under His arm pit and lay Him on His cross. Then one soldier stretches out Jesus' arm and places his foot on the palm of His hand while another soldier takes a five inch nail and starts hammering it through Jesus' wrist. The pain makes Jesus writhe in agony, but not one cry of protest is heard. Instead He is heard to whisper a prayer, "Father forgive them for they know not what they do". The soldier does the same to his other wrist and with one last nail secures His feet to the cross.

However did Jesus endure this terrible pain quietly? If we get so much as a thorn or a needle to prick our finger we cry 'Ouch', and let everyone know the pain we're going through. Will we ever be as brave as you? Whenever we think lightly of sin, let's remember the pain Jesus went through to have our sins forgiven. We must try never to hate those people who harm us, but love them and pray for them, as Jesus did.

We pray for the people who hurt and harm us. May Jesus help us to forgive then and try not to get our own back.

12. JESUS DIES ON HIS CROSS

For three hours Jesus has been hanging on His cross. The sky is darkening and it looks as if a storm is about to break. The whole of nature seems to be weeping for Jesus. His Mother and His friends have never left His side. Jesus says to John, His beloved apostle, "This is your mother." and now Our Lady is our mother too. How thoughtful of Jesus. Jesus is very thirsty now, and cries out for a drink. One kind man soaks a sponge in wine that tastes like vinegar, puts it on the end of a stick and holds it up to Jesus' lips. It makes Him feel a bit better, but what He is really thirsty for is our love. One of the thieves crucified with Jesus is grumpy and hasn't a good word to say. He wants Jesus to save him from dying. The other thief recognises Jesus as a king and asks for a place in His kingdom, Jesus in great pain turns His head towards him and promises him paradise that day. Jesus has done perfectly everything God asked Him to do. He has shown his love for us by saving us from the clutches of the Devil. Now His work on earth is finished. All He longs for is to return to His Father in heaven and as He dies He says, "Father, into your hands I commend my Spirit."

We pray for all those who will die today. Like the repentant thief, may they be with Jesus in His kingdom.

13. JESUS IS TAKEN DOWN FROM THE CROSS

Pilate allows Jesus' friend Joseph of Arimathea to take his body down from the cross and bury it. So with the help of another friend, Nicodemus, and John the beloved apostle they gently remove the crown of thorns and the nails which secured Jesus' body to the cross. They place Him in the lap of His mother, and she gently holds Him in her arms, She feels sad now, but she knows that in three days He will rise from the dead and bring joy to her and all who love Him.

Seeing Our Lady weeping, we want to make her happy. We tell her we are sorry for the pain we caused Jesus and her, and we promise her that we will try to be good.

We pray for all our true friends, who help us when we need them, and we thank God for all the love they give us.

14. JESUS IS PLACED IN THE TOMB

Mary and the other women hastily anoint the body of Jesus for in a very short while the Sabbath begins and they will not be allowed to do any work. When the anointing is finished the men carry Jesus' body to the tomb which Joseph of Arimathea had prepared for himself. This was Joseph's last gift to Jesus. There Jesus is laid and it takes the great strength of the three men to roll the huge stone against the entrance of the tomb. It is a very sad moment for Jesus' friends. As they leave, guards arrive at the tomb to make sure that none of His disciples steal His body.

We know that on Easter Sunday Jesus kept His promise and rose from the dead. If we do our best to live good lives, we shall one day be with Him in heaven.

We pray for all God's children, that we will love Jesus and live happily with Him forever in heaven.

Offering the Way of the Cross for the Holy Souls

St. Thomas Aquinas tells us that the fire of purgatory is equal in intensity to the fire of hell, more dreadful than all the possible sufferings of this earth. Today, we follow the Way of the Cross calling to mind the horrific sufferings of Our Lord. We pray this devotion in reparation for our sins and for our helpless brothers and sisters in purgatory. They plead for our prayers. They are so grateful to us for the least little help we can give them. If only we appreciated the pains of purgatory we would never forget them in their torment.

1. JESUS IS CONDEMNED TO DEATH

Jesus has been interrogated by Caiaphas, Herod and Pilate. He has been mocked, beaten, scourged and crowned with thorns. This is Jesus who, on the last day, will judge the world, but today there is no justice for Him. His trial is a mockery, His judges are prejudiced or cowardly, and there is no charge on which He can be convicted. Yet here He stands, condemned to a death of shame and agony.

Jesus, we know it is our first mortal sins which have signed your death warrant. Our sins are the voices which cry out, "Crucify Him!" Our willingness to commit sin was the consent which Pilate gave to the demands of the crowd. And it is our stubbornness, our impatience, our pride which carry out the sentence.

2. JESUS RECEIVES HIS CROSS

The cross is strong and very heavy, because it has to bear His weight when He reaches Calvary. Jesus receives His cross meekly and gladly, knowing it is to be our salvation. Yet although He has foreseen all His sufferings the shock of the cross falling across His shoulder makes Him stagger.

Jesus, the heavy burden placed on your shoulder is the weight of our sins. It is our wrongdoing which makes you carry this cross to Calvary and leaves you to die on it. Yet, we know that we can be forgiven, because you have told us that you are undergoing this bitter trial to win forgiveness for us.

3. JESUS FALLS THE FIRST TIME BENEATH THE CROSS

Bowed down under the weight of the cross, Jesus slowly begins His journey, amid the jeers and insults of the crowd. His agony in the Garden of Gethsemane was enough to exhaust Him, but that was only the beginning of His sufferings. He puts His whole heart into the task of carrying the cross, but now His strength fails Him and He stumbles and falls.

Jesus, for a moment our sins were stronger than you. We repented of the sins of our early life, and we went on well for a while. Then we were caught off our guard by a new temptation, and we suddenly fell away from your grace. All our good habits seemed to go at once, and it was at that moment that you fell down.

4. JESUS MEETS HIS MOTHER

Jesus is wounded by His fall, but He rises and continues His journey. He is bent down under His cross, but then, looking up, He sees His Mother and for an instant they look at each other. Mary wants to share the sufferings of Her Son by being close to Him, and He is soothed by her sad smile amid the sights and noises of the surrounding crowd. Jesus seems almost unrecognisable now, so changed and deformed by the load of the world's sins which He carries, but He gives His mother a loving, encouraging look. To Mary, His handsome face, once full of divine innocence and peace, now appears disfigured, like that of some guilty outcast. He who knew no sin has been made sin for us.

Jesus, you were innocent but you carried the guilt and punishment for our sins. Yet, what strength you drew from your meeting with your mother. What comfort and sympathy you gave each other. This has to be the saddest meeting that ever took place between mother and Son – neither of you will ever forget this day through all eternity.

5. SIMON OF CYRENE HELPS JESUS TO CARRY HIS CROSS

Jesus' strength fails, and He cannot go on. His executioners don't know what to do. How are they to get Him to Calvary? Their gaze falls on a man by the roadside who looks strong and active. His name is Simon of Cyrene, and he is seized and compelled to carry the cross with Jesus. It is a heavy task and Simon is afraid, but then his heart is touched by the sight of Jesus' sufferings, and so he gladly takes on this job, counting it a privilege.

It is Mary who has brought Jesus this comfort, through her prayer. As His loving mother, she must have prayed that the soldiers would be less hard on Him. Her prayers are answered and a stranger is sent to help Him.

Mary, your prayers carry more weight than any of ours. Holy Mother of God, pray for us and help us to carry our cross. Pray for us, that we shall be able to rise again when we have fallen. Pray for us when we are discouraged and bowed down by sorrow, anxiety, sickness and even despair. Pray for us when we face temptation, and make us conscious of the help of our Guardian Angels.

6. JESUS AND VERONICA

As Jesus plods up the hill, bathed with sweat, a woman sees Him and takes pity on Him. She makes her way through the crowd and wipes His face with a cloth. In reward for her kindness, her cloth retains the impression of Jesus' holy face.

Again, it was Mary's prayers that were heard and Veronica was sent to ease Her Son's pain. Just as Simon was sent to do a man's work. so Veronica now comes to play a woman's role. She hasn't the strength of Simon to help carry the burden of the cross, but she lovingly does for Jesus what little she can.

Lord, may we all be able to help and serve you, each according to our own abilities and situations. We all have our share of temptations, the weariness of living, despondency when things don't go our way, and above all our sin. Grace builds upon nature. With our natural ability you've given us and the healing touch of your holy Sacraments we can be free from sin and pleasing to you.

7. JESUS FALLS THE SECOND TIME

Every step Jesus takes increases the pain of His wounds and He is weakened by loss of blood. Again, his strength fails Him and He falls. This is the reward the Messiah receives from His chosen people. What has He done to deserve it? Jesus, you have fallen because we have fallen again. We could not stand without your grace, and we have lost that grace through neglect. How often we have carried out our religious duties in a formal way, without any real love, sometimes sadly to present an image. We became lukewarm and complacent, coming to church merely from habit, and we thought more of this world than of the world to come.

8. JESUS COMFORTS THE WOMEN OF JERUSALEM

Seeing the sufferings of Jesus, the women are so grief-stricken that they cry out, with no thought of their own safety. Jesus turns to them and says, "Daughters of Jerusalem, weep not over me, but weep for yourselves and for your children."

Jesus, you foresaw, the destruction of Jerusalem and the distress it would cause these mothers. Could it be that you weep for us? Jesus, you are the Lamb of God who willingly atones for the sins of the world. but if we do not struggle against our sins we shall not be able to gain from your sacrifice. Make us conscious of our sinful tendencies and give us courage to fight against them. You are the only one who can drive away evil from our hearts. May your sacrifice not be in vain.

9. JESUS FALLS THE THIRD TIME

Having almost reached the top of Calvary, Jesus is now utterly exhausted and He falls again. He is hauled to His feet and goaded on by the uncaring soldiers.

Jesus thought of us as He dragged Himself up the hill of Calvary. He saw that we would become self-confident and be tempted in new and unexpected ways. We thought we were coping well with our weakness, but

Satan came down on our unguarded side and got the better of us. Trusting in our own strength, we believed it would be easy to get to heaven. This was our pride, and so we fell again.

10. Jesus is stripped of His garments

At last Jesus arrives at the place of His execution. To prepare Him for the cross, the soldiers tear His garments from His bleeding body, displaying Him to the gaze of the onlookers, who scoff and jeer at Him.

Jesus Himself had nothing of which to be ashamed. He endured shame on Calvary so that we might be spared shame at the Last Judgement. How shall we appear then, exposed before God as we truly are? Only Purgatory can strip away the guilt and corruption of our sins and make us fit company for the angels.

11. Jesus is nailed to the cross

The cross is placed on the ground and Jesus is made to lie on it. He lovingly stretches out His arms, waiting for the executioners to come with hammer and nails to fasten His hands to the wood. The blows are struck, the huge nails are driven through His wrists and the blood gushes forth.

As the cross was set upright Jesus offered Himself to His Father as a ransom for the world. The crowd who saw Him hanging there could not understand. The forces of evil were terrified because their power was waning. But in heaven the adoring angels watched in wonder and admiration.

12. Jesus dies on the cross

During the three hours He hangs on the cross Jesus prays for His murderers, promises Paradise to the penitent thief and gives His Blessed Mother into John's care. Then, all is finished and He bows His head and gives His spirit into the hands of His Father.

Jesus died to save us from sin. Let us put ourselves into God's hands completely and make the salvation of our souls our priority. We will try to detest sin now, as much as we have ever loved it in the past. We will try to break the habits of sin and make an effort to pray regularly, so that with

God's grace we can overcome temptation. If we can die to sin, Jesus will not have died for us in vain.

13. JESUS IS TAKEN DOWN FROM THE CROSS

The crowd have gone home, and Calvary is silent and deserted. Only Jesus' mother, Mary, remains, with John and the two holy women. Now Joseph of Arimathea and Nicodemus arrive. They take down Jesus' body from the cross and lay it in Mary's arms.

Mary's heart was pierced with a sword, as Simeon had foretold. Jesus had left her home as a strong mature man. He was given back to her, mutilated, tortured and crucified. Yet, what sustained Mary through all her sorrow was the greater joy of knowing that He would rise from the dead. As the risen Saviour He would never be parted from her again.

14. JESUS IS LAID IN THE TOMB

For three days Jesus is hidden from Mary. His friends gently take Him from her and He is buried with dignity and honour. The tomb is sealed, and Jesus is left to sleep in peace, awaiting the resurrection.

Is He sleeping in peace? We know that He went to tell souls like Joseph, His foster father, that the time for them to reap their reward in heaven was imminent.

We pray that we may sleep in peace until our resurrection. How many of us can say that when we die we shall go straight to heaven? I think, not many. We most definitely do not want to go to the other unmentionable place. So, we know that we will have a spell, may be a very lengthy one, in purgatory. We hope that our friends will have Masses said for us and that they will remember us in their prayers so that we may soon be released. We look forward to being welcomed into heaven by Our Lady and all the saints.

CONCLUSION

Jesus, we thank you for what you endured for us on Calvary. Through this journey which we have made with you may many souls be released from purgatory. We ask these souls to pray for us now, and help us when we come to serve our time in purgatory.

Vices and virtues on the road to Calvary

INTRODUCTION

As we make the Stations of the Cross, let us remember that at every stage of that journey Jesus encountered His fellow men and women. He knew their weaknesses and their strengths, their vices and their virtues. The forces of good and evil are always in conflict. We witness that conflict on the road to Calvary. What the crucifixion, death, and resurrection of Jesus tell us is that good will always overcome evil.

1.   JESUS IS CONDEMNED TO DEATH

The vice of cowardice was there when Pilate condemned Jesus to death. He knew that Jesus was innocent and did not deserve to die. If Pilate had been a real man he would have made a stand against the accusers of Jesus and seen justice done.

In contrast, the virtue of courage was present in Jesus accepting His sentence and the cruelty that was to follow. He acted purely out of love for us, never spared a thought on Himself, while Pilate thought only of his own safety.

Prayer: Heavenly Father, give us courage to be on the side of truth and never be cowards. When we face difficult trails and challenges to our faith, may we be brave enough to acknowledge you and be your true witnesses.

2.   JESUS RECEIVES HIS CROSS

When the cross was laid on Jesus' shoulders, not only did He accept it willingly and gladly, but He embraced it.

Our reaction is often very different. When the going is hard and our crosses are heavy we moan and groan and grumble, and accept our cross in very poor spirit.

Prayer: Jesus, whenever the cross is difficult to bear, may the picture of you embracing your cross inspire us to carry ours without complaint. We remember that God's will is our peace and is always the best for us.

3. JESUS FALLS THE FIRST TIME

Jesus was a man like us, and in His human frailty He fell under the burden of His cross. How many of us having received His word, welcome it at once with joy. But when some trial or persecution comes we fall away at once. Like the seed that fell among the rocks the word cannot take root and so withers away, achieving nothing. By rising from His fall Jesus encourages us to rise from our sins and to continue our journey of faith.

Prayer: Jesus, deepen our attachment to your word. Keep encouraging us, because we need to hear your words, "Sin no more, go in peace."

4. JESUS MEETS HIS MOTHER

It was hard for Mary to watch her Son on this journey. Once again she had to be obedient to the will of the Father, for it was His will that His Son should die and rise from the grave to save mankind.

In Mary we see the contrast with our first parents, Adam and Eve, who disobeyed God. Through Adam, sin came into the world, and through Jesus sin is conquered.

Prayer: Heavenly Father, may the obedience of Jesus and Mary inspire us to be obedient and to have respect for authority. In our world of rebellion against authority, let us never live in a lawless way, but acknowledge that all authority comes from you.

5. THE CROSS IS LAID UPON SIMON OF CYRENE

Simon is bullied and forced into carrying Jesus' cross. At first there is resentment and reluctance on his part, but he witnesses the goodness of Jesus and his attitude changes. Now he shows brotherly love, a desire to give assistance to someone in need.

Prayer: Heavenly Father, we plead with you to change the hearts of bullies and those who terrorise others. We hold up to you the victims of such treatment, and ask you to fill our world with generous people whose aim is always to love and help those in need.

6.   VERONICA WIPES THE FACE OF JESUS

Veronica's virtue was to show Jesus compassion. She saw His face, bathed in sweat, streaked with blood and dirt, and she realised that she could bring Him a moment's relief. She could have turned away and ignored Jesus' plight, but she braved the execution squad to help Him.

Prayer: Heavenly Father, may we, like Veronica, be people full of compassion. When we see the needs of others may we respond to them. Forgive us for the times when we have been neglectful and failed to notice them.

7.   JESUS FALLS THE SECOND TIME

With every step Jesus weakens and He falls again. At this second fall, we think of the seed which fell among thorns and was choked by them. Many people hear the wisdom of Jesus and accept His words with enthusiasm, but become easily distracted. Greed, the pleasures of this life and materialism choke the word and so they fall away.

Prayer: Heavenly Father, may we always be receptive to the words of your Son. Let us not become so attached to the things of this world that we lose all sense of direction and prevent the word from taking root in our lives.

8.   THE WOMEN OF JERUSALEM MOURN FOR JESUS

Most of the people in that crowd of onlookers were merely interested spectators. They cared nothing for Jesus as He made His painful way towards Calvary, but these women of Jerusalem who wept for Him were full of sympathy.

Prayer: Heavenly Father, may we be sensitive enough to feel for others in distress. We may not be able to offer practical help, but we can be sympathetic, giving our time, our love, and perhaps a shoulder to cry on.

9. Jesus falls the third time

Jesus falls a third time, but He does not give in to weakness. He gets to His feet and carries on, giving us an example of perseverance. He must be heartened by the thought of those people who hear His words and act on them, like the seed which yielded a harvest, thirtyfold, sixtyfold and a hundredfold.

Prayer: Heavenly Father, Satan greatest weapon is discouragement. He is happy when we sees us throwing in the towel when the going is hard. At these times may the perseverance of Jesus inspire and lift us to plod on to the bitter end.

10. Jesus is stripped of His garments

The soldiers who strip Jesus of His garments show their complete contempt for Him and indifference to His feelings. There are many people who treat their fellow human beings in this way, regarding them as objects of lust and self-gratification. St. Paul tells us that the body is the temple of the Holy Spirit and should be respected.

Prayer: Heavenly Father, may we be pure in thought, word and deed. Help us to encourage in our world the virtues of chastity and respect for others.

11. Jesus is nailed to the cross

The men who nailed Jesus to His cross were brutal and barbaric. They too were victims, for by their repeated acts of cruelty they brutalised all the good in their nature. Our consciences, too, can become hardened and insensitive, so that we gradually lose all awareness of sin. The more often we commit the same sin, the more easily we live with it, and cease to recognise it as sin.

Prayer: Heavenly Father, give us a love for you that is deep and sensitive. May we never silence our conscience by becoming immune to the cruelty and evil we experience all around us.

12. JESUS DIES ON THE CROSS

As Jesus suffered on the cross, He experienced the loyalty of His mother and His beloved disciple, John. They stayed close to Him to the very end. Although their hearts were broken they could never have left Him. Jesus witnessed, too, the virtue of repentance in the Good Thief. He had an open mind to receive the call of Jesus and repent of all his wrongdoing.

Prayer: Heavenly Father, through our Baptism we are called to a life of fidelity. But in our path there are many obstacles to face; the wiles of Satan, the allurements of the world, the pleasures of the flesh to mention just a few. Your grace can help us to remain steadfast and faithful, but should we fall you are always there to reward our repentance.

13. JESUS IS TAKEN DOWN FROM THE CROSS

The soldiers nailed Jesus to the cross with such crudeness and cruelty. Now we witness Joseph of Arimathea, Nicodemus and John, the beloved disciple take down the body of Jesus from the cross with the utmost kindness and gentleness. They place it in the lap of Mary His mother who receives it with heartfelt sadness.

Prayer: Heavenly Father, in every walk of life bullies are to be found. Also people who lack respect for the feelings of others and who walk all over them. May we remember the words of your Son who said, "Learn from me for I am gentle and humble in heart."

14. JESUS IS LAID IN THE SEPULCHRE

It was the kindness of Nicodemus that provided Jesus with the most costly ointment and fine linen cloth for His burial. It was the generosity of Joseph of Arimathea that furnished Jesus with a worthy tomb.

Prayer: Heavenly Father, the source of all generosity, from whom all good things come, take away from our hearts all greed and covetousness. Make us aware of the needs of others and be always ready to share what we have with the poor and needy.

CONCLUSION

We have witnessed all the vices and virtues that were present at Calvary. Vice brought out all the ugliness to be found in our nature. Virtue displayed the beauty that can be found in our lives. Heavenly Father, free will is your gift to us. We can choose to be either virtuous and good or vicious and evil. Give us the grace to lead virtuous lives and to abhor vice of all kind. When we are surrounded on all sides by evil, let us remember that the good we attempt is never lost for good always overcomes evil. We thank you for giving us your Son Jesus and for the great sacrifice He made on our behalf. May we express our gratitude by leading good lives worthy of His love.

With Jesus we suffer, with Jesus we are healed

1. JESUS IS CONDEMNED TO DEATH

Jesus was betrayed by a friend, accused by false witnesses and sentenced to a punishment He did not deserve.

When we are hurt by others, betrayed, or treated unjustly let us turn to Jesus who will help us to cope with our situation.

2. JESUS RECEIVES HIS CROSS

In accepting His cross Jesus took on the burden of our sin in order to save us from evil.

He is the Lamb of God who takes away all the sin of the world. Let us ask Him to heal us of the damage caused by sin.

3. JESUS FALLS THE FIRST TIME

Jesus had scarcely started His journey and the unexpected weight of that cross made Him stagger and fall.

Sometimes we fall into sin through carelessness. Let us ask Jesus to make us more aware of danger, and when we do fall may we be just as quick to return to Him and ask for forgiveness.

4. JESUS MEETS HIS MOTHER

Mary, the mother of Jesus, shared so much of His life, and she shared His sufferings, too.

Let us pray that she will console all those mothers whose children are taken from them by a sudden or violent death.

5. THE CROSS IS LAID UPON SIMON OF CYRENE

Simon was called upon to help Jesus bear His cross. We too, are called upon to share each other's burdens and troubles. Let us ask Jesus to give us the patience to help others, knowing that what we do for them we are doing for Him.

6. VERONICA WIPES THE FACE OF JESUS

Veronica saw Jesus passing by, covered with dirt, sweat and blood, and she brought Him momentary relief by bathing His face.

Let us pray that Jesus will bless and reward every act of kindness, however small.

7. JESUS FALLS THE SECOND TIME

Pain and exhaustion took their toll on Jesus and He fell to His knees again.

Sometimes we fall into sin because others cause us to fall. We are deceived, tempted, bullied, led astray. Let us ask Jesus to give us the strength to withstand temptation and resist the attractions of sin. May we never forget that His forgiveness and healing are offered to us to help us continue our journey.

8. JESUS MEETS THE WOMEN OF JERUSALEM

The women of Jerusalem wept for Jesus. They saw Him being led away to His death, and they felt so helpless.

Let us go to Jesus when we are in distress or sorrow, remembering that the Lord is close to the broken-hearted.

9. JESUS FALLS THE THIRD TIME

Jesus was nearing the end of His journey. He knew that worse suffering was about to begin, and the thought of it made Him fall once more.

Sometimes our sins are serious and deliberate. Then we feel such remorse and despair that there seems no point in carrying on. We pray that with the help of Jesus we will never lose heart. No matter how often or how far we have fallen, He is always waiting to forgive us and lift us up again.

10. JESUS IS STRIPPED OF HIS GARMENTS

When Jesus reached Calvary the soldiers roughly removed His clothing in preparation for crucifixion. He was naked and humiliated in front of a crowd of onlookers.

Whenever we are rejected or exposed to ridicule, may we feel the presence of Jesus giving us strength.

11. JESUS IS NAILED TO THE CROSS

Jesus wanted to share our human suffering so He allowed Himself to be nailed to the cross.

Let us pray that He will help us to endure physical pain and sickness, and accept those sufferings which we cannot avoid.

12. JESUS DIES ON THE CROSS

Greater than any physical pain was the spiritual anguish of separation from God, which made Jesus cry out, "My God, why have you forsaken me?"

When we feel lost, abandoned, and far away from God, let us look at Jesus on the cross and remember that His death reconciled us with our loving Father in heaven.

13. JESUS IS TAKEN DOWN FROM THE CROSS

The body of Jesus was taken down from the cross by His loving and generous friends and was gently placed in Mary's arms.

It is hard to come to terms with the loss of a loved one. We pray that Jesus will comfort those who mourn, wipe away their tears, and surround them with kindness.

14. JESUS IS LAID IN THE TOMB

After His earthly life was over, Jesus was buried in a secure tomb. We believe that on the third day He rose to a new life.

We pray that Jesus will give us the grace to put the sins of our past life behind us, to forgive ourselves, and to look forward to each new day.

CONCLUSION

Jesus, in your life and in your death you showed your love and compassion for all mankind. Show us how we can share your sufferings. May we one day rise with you in glory. Until that day may be experience your healing power in our lives and continue your work in our damaged world.

Praising Jesus every step of the Way

(based on the 14 Divine Praises)

Has it ever struck you that there are fourteen Divine Praises? Each of them can be used as a meditation on a Station of the Cross. In making the Way of the Cross with Jesus we will first set the scene of each Station and then pray for people in various needs.

1. JESUS IS CONDEMNED TO DEATH

Blessed be God.

Jesus, having been scourged and mocked is now sentenced to the most cruel death, death on a cross. Jesus isn't just a man, He is the Son of God, and He comes to do God's will. All His sufferings are part of God's plan, for God so loved us that He sent His only Son into the world so that all who believe in Him should have life.

Let us pray for all those who find God's will for themselves so hard. They seem to think that God is asking too much of them. If only they would believe that God's will is our peace and that God our Father only wishes the best for us. Blessed be God.

2. JESUS RECEIVES HIS CROSS

Blessed be His Holy Name.

The soldiers treat Jesus with the utmost contempt, callously placing the heavy cross on His shoulders and ordering Him to carry it to the place of execution. They do not know who He really is, so they show Him no respect.

We pray for all those who have no respect for God and use His name carelessly, irreverently or maliciously. Blessed be His Holy Name.

3.   Jesus falls the first time

Blessed be Jesus Christ, true God and true man.

Jesus was born into our world, a man like us in all things but sin. He lived and died as a man, and in His human weakness He falls under the intolerable burden of the cross. But He is also God, and because He is God made man He is able to save us from our sins.

Jesus said, "To have seen me is to have seen the Father". We pray that we may all have a closer relationship with Jesus, and through Him be closer to our heavenly Father. Blessed be Jesus Christ, true God and true man.

4.   Jesus meets His mother

Blessed be the name of Jesus.

With what mixed feelings Mary sees her Son approaching. She is heartbroken to see Him suffering, but she knows that He is doing His Father's will and she is proud to be a part of it. She thinks back to a time before He was born, when the angel came to tell her that she was chosen to bear a very special child who was to be called Jesus. Now, all the prophecies are being fulfiled, and Jesus is about to complete His work on earth.

Mary always spoke the name of Jesus with great love and affection. No one would have voiced His name as she did. The name of Jesus, is unique and powerful. He told His disciples that whatever they asked in His name they would receive. We pray that we may always have confidence in the name of Jesus. May we carry His name in our hearts and often call upon it in love and whenever we are in trouble or temptation. Blessed be the name of Jesus.

5.   The cross is laid upon Simon of Cyrene

Blessed be His Most Sacred Heart.

Jesus is unable to carry His cross alone, and so a stranger, Simon of Cyrene, is dragged out of the crowd and made to help Him. At first Simon tries to refuse, but he feels pity for this poor prisoner. Jesus, with tender love in His heart, draws Simon to Him and changes him from a reluctant conscript into a willing helper.

We pray for all those who are trying to carry a heavy cross. May they understand that they are never alone, that Jesus' heart is full of love for them. Blessed be His Most Sacred Heart.

6. VERONICA WIPES THE FACE OF JESUS

Blessed be His Most Precious Blood.

Jesus is showing the strain of His ordeal, and Veronica wants to do what she can to ease His pain and discomfort. She brings a clean towel and begins to wipe His face, bathing away the sweat and blood. His blood, which Jesus is going to shed on the cross, leaves an imprint of His face on Veronica's towel. How she must have treasured that gift from Jesus!

We pray for those who are discouraged by the thought of their sins, and those who can't believe that God can forgive them. May they remember that Jesus has washed away all sin by shedding His precious blood. Blessed be His Most Precious Blood.

7. JESUS FALLS THE SECOND TIME

Blessed be Jesus in the most holy Sacrament of the altar.

Jesus is struggling to bear the heavy load of the world's sins. He is aware of the powerful forces of evil which surround Him, and in His distress He falls again. It is His love for us, His determination to offer Himself in sacrifice for us, that inspires Him to get to His feet and continue the journey.

Satan is active in our world until the end of time. Our greatest weapon against him is the presence of Jesus. We possess the presence of Jesus when two or more of us are gathered together in prayer, in the Scriptures, but particularly in the most Blessed Sacrament of the altar. Jesus, may we give you the respect that is due to you in the Blessed Sacrament. Blessed be Jesus in the most holy Sacrament of the altar.

8.   JESUS MEETS THE WOMEN OF JERUSALEM

Blessed be the Holy Spirit, the Paraclete.

The women of Jerusalem weep for Jesus in love and sympathy. He is their friend and they cannot bear to lose Him. Jesus tells them not to weep for Him but for themselves and their children, because of the hardships that lie ahead of them.

Jesus promised that He would not leave us orphans but would send us a Comforter, His Holy Spirit. We pray for all those who feel unloved, those who grieve for a loved one, those lost and alone in the world. May they all receive the comfort and warmth of the Holy Spirit. Blessed be the Holy Spirit, the Paraclete.

9.   JESUS FALLS THE THIRD TIME

Blessed be the great Mother of God. Mary most holy.

Jesus' strength is now at its lowest ebb. The cross seems to be getting heavier with every step and He falls again. Glancing up He sees His mother. Her look encourages Him to rise to His feet.

Mary is our mother too. She is concerned with all we do. Her one desire is our happiness and she wants us to be with the Blessed Trinity and herself in heaven. When we fall she is always there to encourage us with a mother's love. We pray for the grace to be more aware of Mary's love and to ask for her encouragement in our lives. Blessed be the great Mother of God, Mary most holy.

10. JESUS IS STRIPPED OF HIS GARMENTS

Blessed be her holy and Immaculate Conception.

Jesus, though innocent, now suffers the punishment of being stripped of His clothing and exhibited to a mocking crowd. His innocent mother has to witness this additional insult to her beloved Son.

There have only been two sinless people in this world, Jesus and Mary. Satan could never gain any control over them. How difficult it is to maintain childlike innocence in a corrupt world, but Jesus tells us if we wish to enter the kingdom of heaven we must be like little children. We pray for young people, that they will preserve their purity in spite of all temptations. Jesus says of them, "See that you never despise any of these little ones, for their angels in heaven are continually in the presence of my Father." We pray for all those who try to pervert the innocent, that Our Lady will purify their hearts and minds. Blessed be her holy and Immaculate Conception.

11. JESUS IS NAILED TO THE CROSS

Blessed be Her Glorious Assumption.

Nails are hammered into the wrists and feet of Jesus. What excruciating pain Jesus endured for us! To careless passers-by this is simply the shameful execution of a criminal. Yet Jesus knows the rewards that are to come. He looks forward to His own reward, His reunion with His Father in heaven. He foresees also the crown which will be given to His Blessed Mother in that kingdom

We pray that we may accept our sorrows and our problems as a means to salvation. Mary was richly and justly rewarded for co-operating with God's will. May we be comforted and encouraged by the promise of our reward to come. Blessed be Her Glorious Assumption.

12. JESUS DIES ON THE CROSS

Blessed be the name of Mary, Virgin and Mother.

As Jesus hangs on His cross in pain and exhaustion He thinks of us, the people He loves. He thinks especially of His beloved mother, Mary, and the part she has played in the redemption of all sinners. He chooses this moment, just as He is about to die, to ask Mary to be John's mother. In so doing, He makes her the mother of us all.

We pray that we may always be close to Mary, our mother, and make a place of honour for her in our lives, as John did. Blessed be the name of Mary, Virgin and Mother.

13. JESUS IS TAKEN DOWN FROM THE CROSS

Blessed be St. Joseph, her spouse most chaste.

Now the friends of Jesus come to take down His body from the cross, and Mary cradles Him in her arms. The women begin the anointing of Jesus' body, working quickly because of the approaching Sabbath.

Death is something we shall all have to face, and it can be a frightening prospect. St. Joseph has been given the title, 'Patron of the Dying' because Mary and Jesus were present at his death. If we fear dying let us call upon Joseph. May we all be given the grace of a happy death. Jesus, Mary and Joseph, remember me in my last agony. Blessed be St. Joseph, her spouse most chaste.

14. JESUS IS BURIED

Blessed be God in His angels and in His saints.

With heavy hearts the mother and friends of Jesus carry Him to the tomb of Joseph of Arimathea in a nearby garden, and there He is laid to rest. The entrance to the tomb is sealed with a large stone.

On the third day, the women returned to the tomb and found that the stone had been rolled away and the body of Jesus was no longer there. Two angels appeared, saying to them, "Why look among the dead for someone who is alive? He is not here; He has risen." Angels play a large part in our lives. We all have a guardian angel to guide and protect us. May we constantly be aware of their presence. The saints too should be prominent in our lives. They are given to us as models to show us how to persevere. May we follow their example and rise in glory with them and Jesus on the last day. Blessed be God in His angels and in His saints.

CONCLUSION

Jesus, we thank you for allowing us to spend a little time with you, sharing your journey to Calvary and meditating on the mysteries of our faith. However can we thank you for the depth of your love for us? All you ask of us is that we love you in return. May we all one day live with the Father, the Son and Holy Spirit; with Mary and Joseph and all your angels and saints.

Following the Messiah to Calvary

INTRODUCTION

Scripture foretold that the Messiah would come as a suffering servant who would be despised and rejected and would die for His people. Let us follow the Way of the Cross today, considering how Jesus fulfiled the prophecies and offered Himself for us as the sacrificial lamb.

1. JESUS IS CONDEMNED TO DEATH

"By force and by law He was taken; would anyone plead His cause?" [Isaiah 53 v.8]

We think of Jesus being seized by the high priest's guards and then being interrogated by Caiaphas, Herod and Pilate. False witnesses were brought against him. No-one defended Him, nor did He defend Himself.

Comment. The powerful of this world have money and 'friends' to support them while the weak are alone and helpless. If we take pity on the weak, it is Jesus we are defending.

2. JESUS RECEIVES HIS CROSS

"Ours were the sufferings He bore, ours the sorrows He carried." [Isaiah 53 v.4]

We think of Jesus taking on the heavy burden of our sin. Though He was innocent, He was willing to accept this punishment on our behalf.

Comment. Jesus took responsibility for our salvation. We have but one life to save, may we take responsibility for that life.

3. JESUS FALLS THE FIRST TIME

"Harshly dealt with, He bore it humbly, He never opened His mouth." [Isaiah 53 v.7]

We think of Jesus, falling under the weight of the cross, goaded by the soldiers, but never once complaining.

Comment. When others place burdens on us we complain and sometimes retaliate. We fail to use that burden as a means of spiritual growth.

4. JESUS MEETS HIS MOTHER

"The Lord called me before I was born, from my mother's womb. He pronounced my name. Does a woman forget her baby, or fail to cherish the son of her womb?" [Isaiah 49 v.1.15]

How could Mary ever forget that visit from the angel, announcing that she was to be the mother of the Messiah? How could she forget the birth of her beloved son in Bethlehem? She must have shared so many memories with Jesus when she met Him on His last sorrowful journey.

Comment. Do we remember the debt we owe our own mothers? Do we pray for them and long to be with them in heaven like Jesus longed for His mother to join Him?

5. THE CROSS IS LAID UPON SIMON OF CYRENE

"Trouble is near, I have no-one to help me." [Psalm 22 v.11]

We think of Jesus struggling to carry that heavy cross all alone. But He was not left completely alone, for Simon came forward to help Him and to lighten the burden.

Comment. There are many lonely people in this world who have no one to help them carry their burdens. Do we recognise them and give them an arm to lean on and a shoulder to cry on?

6. VERONICA WIPES THE FACE OF JESUS

"Without beauty, without majesty, no looks to attract our eyes." [Isaiah 53 v.2]

All the agony of Jesus – pain, exhaustion, the heat of the day must have shown in His face. No doubt He was frowning in pain, and His face would be smeared with blood and dirt. Yet Veronica saw a suffering human being, took pity on Him, and bathed His face clean.

Comment. Often it is hard to see beyond appearances to the real person. In doing this we fail to help them and so fail to see Jesus in them.

7.   JESUS FALLS THE SECOND TIME

"The Lord has been pleased to crush Him with suffering." [Isaiah 53 v 10]

We think of Jesus falling again under that intolerable burden. Only His determination to do His father's will and achieve His purpose kept Him going.

Comment. How often we fail to see that suffering has a good purpose. This is where Jesus is our example because He brought so much good out of His suffering.

8.   JESUS MEETS THE WOMEN OF JERUSALEM

"Shout for joy, you barren women who bore no children!" [isaiah 54 v.1]

We think of Jesus telling the weeping women not to concern themselves with Him but with their own troubles, which He clearly foresaw. Jerusalem was to be destroyed, and many mothers would have cause to weep for their families.

Comment. Jesus is teaching us here that the way to cope with a burden is to help other people with theirs. If only we would try to follow His example!

9.   JESUS FALLS THE THIRD TIME

"A thing despised and rejected by men, a man of sorrows and familiar with suffering." [Isaiah 53 v.3]

We think of Jesus on His knees in the dust once again The crowd looked at Him with contempt, seeing only a worthless criminal going to his death. How alone Jesus must have felt.

Comment. Coping with rejection is painful. We all look for recognition and friendship. When we are crushed and alone may we picture Jesus in the same plight and remember He will never reject us.

10. JESUS IS STRIPPED OF HIS GARMENTS

"They divide my garments among them, they cast lots for my clothes." [Psalm 22 v.18]

We think of Jesus experiencing the indignity of having His clothes stripped from Him. Then those Roman soldiers threw dice for His cloak.

Comment. At times we can be cruel and unfeeling, profiting from other people's misfortunes. Instead of sympathising with them we try to turn the situation to our advantage.

11. JESUS IS NAILED TO THE CROSS

"He was pierced through for our faults." [isaiah 53 v.5]

We think of Jesus enduring the terrible pain of being nailed to the cross. All the time He was thinking of us.

Comment. May we think of Jesus whenever we sin. Every sin is a hammer blow causing Him intense pain.

12. JESUS DIES ON THE CROSS

"My God, my God, why have your forsaken me?" [Psalm 22 v.1]

We think of how desolate Jesus must have felt as He hung on the cross. He even felt deserted by His Father in heaven and He cried out to Him in anguish.

Comment. Surely separation from God is the greatest possible pain! May we remember that in our darkest hour God never deserts us.

13. JESUS IS TAKEN DOWN FROM THE CROSS

"His soul's anguish over, He shall see the light and be content." [Isaiah 53 v.11]

We think of Jesus' mother and His friends coming to take down His body from the cross. They were sorrowful, but thankful that His sufferings were over and that He had accomplished His task.

Comment. For Mary the death of Jesus was not the end. It was the beginning of hope in the life to come. When life is hard may we look for brighter days if not in this world, most certainly in the next.

14. Jesus is buried

"They gave him a tomb with the rich." [Isaiah 53 v.9]

We think of that generous friend of Jesus, Joseph of Arimathea, who gave his own tomb as a burial place for his Master. The Messiah who was born in a poor stable was buried in a rich man's tomb.

Comment. There will always be people worse off than ourselves. May we never fail to offer them help from our store of good things.

Conclusion

We thank Jesus for fulfilling the prophecies written about Him. Knowing what He had to do made it all the harder for Him. Still He never flinched. May we appreciate the great sacrifice He made for us. We remember the words of Isaiah, "On him lies a punishment that brings us peace, and through his wounds we are healed."

Jesus shows the Way

1. JESUS IS CONDEMNED TO DEATH

Jesus, you were cruelly sentenced to death, but you accepted that sentence without protest. Help us to accept patiently whatever suffering we may have to face.

2. JESUS RECEIVES HIS CROSS

Jesus, you loved us so much that you were willing to take up the cross and pay the price of our sins. Help us to repent of those sins. Show us how we should accept and carry the crosses we are given.

3. JESUS FALLS THE FIRST TIME

Jesus, the weight of the cross caused you to fall, but you were determined to get to your feet and carry on. Help us never to be discouraged when we fall, but to follow your example and overcome the obstacles in our way.

4. JESUS MEETS HIS MOTHER

Jesus, your Mother shared your agony and comforted you. May we always remember that she is our mother, too. She loves us, she feels all our sorrows and she is ready to comfort us when we turn to her.

5. SIMON OF CYRENE HELPS TO CARRY THE CROSS

Jesus, when you were struggling alone with your burden, a stranger came to help you. May we respond generously wherever we see a friend or a stranger needing help.

6. VERONICA WIPES THE FACE OF JESUS

Jesus, you were grateful to Veronica for her small, but brave act of kindness. Teach us to recognise you in other people and treat them kindly for your sake.

7. JESUS FALLS THE SECOND TIME

Jesus, you were so weakened by your ordeal that you fell a second time. When we are weakened by temptation, give us some of your strength so that, with your help, we can continue our journey by your side.

8. JESUS MEETS THE WOMEN OF JERUSALEM

Jesus, although you were exhausted and in pain, you made the effort to speak to these distressed women. Help us to follow your example of unselfishness, putting aside our own troubles when other people need our sympathy.

9. JESUS FALLS THE THIRD TIME

Jesus, the terrible sight of Calvary so near made you fall once more. When we are afraid, help us to trust you and rely on you to sustain us.

10. JESUS IS STRIPPED OF HIS GARMENTS

Jesus, to prepare you for crucifixion your executioners stripped away your clothing. May we learn to be detached from all that is inessential in our lives, so that we may grow closer to you.

11. JESUS IS NAILED TO THE CROSS

Jesus, the pain you suffered in being nailed by your hands and feet to the cross is difficult for us to imagine. When we have to suffer pain of any kind, give us some of your courage and endurance. Show us how to unite our sufferings with yours.

12. JESUS DIES ON THE CROSS

Jesus, you died a brutal and painful death to save us from the power of evil. Make us always grateful to you for what you have done for us. Help us to show our gratitude in the lives we live.

13. JESUS IS TAKEN DOWN FROM THE CROSS

Jesus, your wounded body was treated reverently and lovingly by your Mother and your faithful friends. Teach us to have respect and love for your body and blood which we receive in the Blessed Sacrament.

14. JESUS IS LAID IN THE TOMB

Jesus, on the third day you rose from your tomb and conquered death. We pray that we shall one day rise to everlasting life with you.

He suffered, died and rose for us

1. JESUS IS CONDEMNED TO DEATH

Jesus stands before Pilate accused as a blasphemer, a disturber of the peace, and one who claims to be an earthly king. On all such charges He is condemned. He is innocent.

How many people like Jesus have been unjustly condemned and have no-one to appeal their innocence! Jesus understands how they must feel. May they turn to Him for comfort.

2. JESUS RECEIVES HIS CROSS

The heavy cross is laid upon the shoulders of Jesus.

How many times people have had to carry a cross they find too heavy! May they turn to Jesus for consolation.

3. JESUS FALLS THE FIRST TIME

Jesus is physically weak and the weight of the cross makes Him stumble and fall

How many people fall into sin at an early stage of their lives, through being led astray, lack of experience, ignorance and, sadly, malice! May they not be discouraged but look at Jesus getting to His feet and so be helped to continue their journey through life.

4. Jesus meets His afflicted Mother

Mary is there to comfort her Son in His suffering and sorrow.

How many mothers see their children suffer before their eyes! If they are inconsolable and helpless may they see how Mary suffered on this painful journey and seek comfort from her.

5. Simon of Cyrene helps Jesus to carry His cross

The cross is too heavy for Jesus, and Simon is made to help Jesus carry it.

How many times we have had a cross too heavy to carry and Jesus has given us someone like Simon to carry or share the load! May we not fail to express our gratitude.

6. Veronica wipes the face of Jesus

The thoughtful and courageous Veronica, by wiping the face of Jesus brings Him some comfort and love.

How many times in life we have met people who have been thoughtful and brave enough to go out of their way to ease our sufferings! May we not take their efforts for granted but ask Jesus to shower them with His choicest blessings.

7. Jesus falls the second time

Half way through the painful journey to Calvary Jesus falls again.

How many people fall away from the Lord through some middle age crisis, be it in their marriage, or boredom in their vocation! May this fall of Jesus' at the middle of his journey to Calvary inspire them to pick themselves up and bravely continue on their journey through life.

8. The women of Jerusalem mourn for Jesus

Some women are moved by compassion to weep at the sight of Jesus' sufferings.

How many times in our lives there have been moments of failure and bereavement and there have been people who have comforted and encouraged us! May we be like them and help others we may find in the same plight.

9. JESUS FALLS THE THIRD TIME

Jesus has nearly reached the hill of Calvary and He falls for the last time.

How many people at the end of their lives have been tempted to give up trying and not persevere to the end! We pray for them, and may we all be given the grace of final perseverance.

10. JESUS IS STRIPPED OF HIS GARMENTS

The soldiers roughly strip Jesus of His garments. The pain is excruciating.

How many people have unashamedly exposed themselves through malice or profit and so have degraded themselves and corrupted or offended others! May this stripping of Jesus find them forgiveness.

11. JESUS IS NAILED TO HIS CROSS

The nails are hammered through the hands and feet of Jesus to secure Him to His cross. He endures this pain willingly.

How many people have had to endure excruciating suffering, like Jesus' nailing to the cross! May the thought of Jesus being nailed to the cross make them realise that He feels for them and will help them to endure their pain.

12. JESUS DIES ON THE CROSS

Jesus in His agony hangs on His cross for three hours. Forgiving His enemies and commending Himself to His Father, He dies.

How many people have reached rock bottom and despaired! May they realise that Jesus on the cross also experienced being abandoned by His Father. Like Jesus, may they commend themselves to the loving arms of our heavenly Father.

13. JESUS IS TAKEN DOWN FROM THE CROSS

Jesus is taken down from the cross and placed in the arms of His Mother

How many mothers have seen their children die through accidents or natural causes! May they find comfort from Mary, who had to hold her dead son in her arms.

14. JESUS IS LAID IN THE SEPULCHRE

Jesus is laid in the tomb. Only His Mother Mary expects the resurrection.

How many mothers have been inconsolable as they bury their children! Mary appreciates how heartbroken they are. May they seek comfort from her.

Biographical Details

Fr. Francis Maple was born in India in 1938 and moved to Britain at the age of ten. He joined the Capuchin Franciscans when he was 17 and since his ordination he has spent most of his life in North Wales and the North West of England. He is the author of two books on the Rosary (a third is planned), a book of children's stories, and three volumes of 'Thoughts' based on the daily column he writes for the Wrexham Evening Leader. He has also published a collection of Sunday sermons on CD.

In addition to his writing, Fr. Francis has made a name for himself as a singer and guitarist, having recorded 31 LP's and has a gold disc for the rendering of the 'Old Rugged Cross'. These skills have raised thousands of pounds for Third World charity projects. In 1997 he was awarded the MBE for his charity work.

While leading a busy life as Guardian and Parish Priest at the Friary in Chester, he manages to find time for a few hobbies, including reading, listening to music, cooking and crochet.